Ian Carroll is a best selling author, with all of h paperback and also on Kindle.

Ian is the author of the 'A-Z of Bloody Horror' titles – *'Warning: Water May Contain Merm Aisle 3'* and *'Pensioner'*. Also the author of tne norror books *'My Name is Ishmael'*, *'Demon Pirates Vs. Vikings – Blackhorn's Revenge'*, *'The Lover's Guide to Internet Dating'* and *'Valentines Day'*.

'Hammer Horror' is also the first book in *'The Movie Fans Have Their Say'* series of Books, with many more planned for the future.

He is also the author of the music books –
'Lemmy: Memories of a Rock 'N' Roll Legend' – which was a #1 in the UK, USA, Canada, France and Germany – *'Ronnie James Dio: Man on the Silver Mountain – Memories of a Rock 'N' Roll Icon'*, *'Leonard Cohen: Just One More Hallelujah'*, *'Music, Mud and Mayhem: The Official History of the Reading Festival'* and *'From Donington to Download: The History of Rock at Donington Park'*.

The First Twelve Volumes of the *'Fans Have Their Say...'* series are also available which are:

'The Fans Have Their Say #1   KISS - We Wanted the Best and We Got the Best'.
'The Fans Have Their Say #2   AC/DC – Rock 'N' Roll From the Land Down Under'.
'The Fans Have Their Say #3   BLACK SABBATH – The Lords of Darkness'.
'The Fans Have Their Say #4   GUNS 'N ROSES – Welcome to the Jungle...'
'The Fans Have Their Say #5   METALLICA – Exit, Light, Enter, Night'
'The Fans Have Their Say #6   QUEEN – Is This the Real Life...?'
'The Fans Have Their Say #7   ELTON JOHN – Count the Headlights on the Highway...'
'The Fans Have Their Say #8   MEAT LOAF – All Revved Up...'
'The Fans Have Their Say #9   DEF LEPPARD – Steel-City Rock Stars'
'The Fans Have Their Say #10 BON JOVI – New Jersey's Finest'
'The Fans Have Their Say #11 CINDERELLA – A Rock 'N' Roll Fairytale'
'The Fans Have Their Say #12 MOTLEY CRUE - L.A. Rock 'n' Roll Bad Boys'

Ian has also written the history section for the Official Reading Festival music site in the UK and has attended the festival 33 times since 1983.

Ian lives with his wife Raine, two sons – Nathan & Josh - plus Stanley and the memories of a jet-black witches cat called Rex - in Plymouth, Devon, UK.

www.iancarrollauthor.com
Facebook.com/iancarrollauthor (Various Book Pages as well)
ian@iancarrollauthor.com

© Ian Carroll 2019

ISBN - 9781653887675

No part of this publication can be reproduced in any form or by any means, electronic or mechanical – including photocopy, recording or via any other retrieval system, without written permission from the Author/Publishers.

All other Photographs/Posters and covers of Whitesnake LP's remain the copyright of the various associated production and distribution companies and are presented here for educative and review purposes only (under 'Fair Use' rules) to spread the knowledge and adoration of this artist and should not be reproduced in any way.

The Fans Have Their Say #13

Whitesnake

In the Still of the Night...

© Ian Carroll 2019

The Fan Have Their Say #13 Whitesnake: In the Still of the Night...

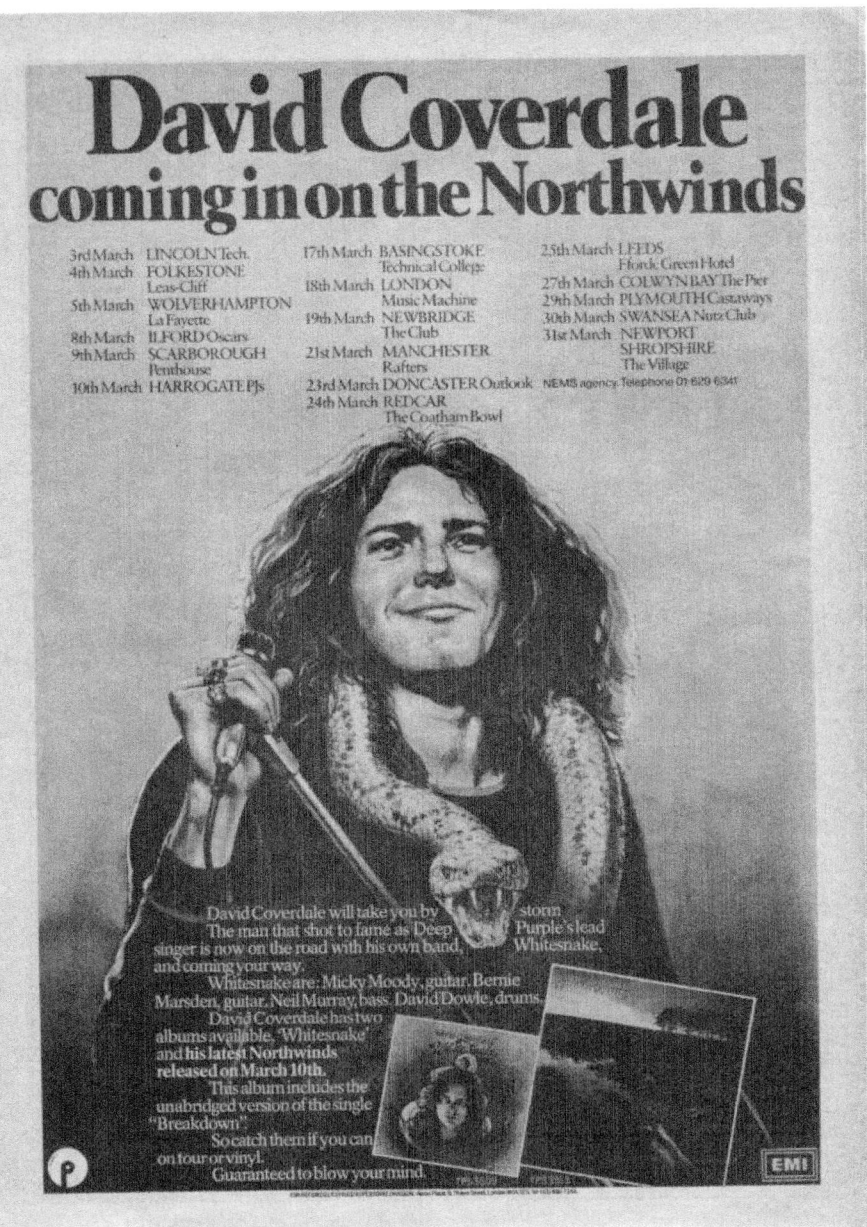

Introduction

Growing up in the 1970's I was subjected, through choice to all sorts of rock and metal music – especially at school and beyond.

I used to have a huge 'ghetto-blaster' back in the day and my 'mates' and me would hang around listening to all the best bands on cassettes, swapping and lending each other the greatest ones and playing them until the tapes stretched and split through use. Our popular choices at the time were:

AC/DC - 'If You Want Blood, You've Got It'
Saxon   - 'Wheels of Steel'
Gillan - 'Glory Road'
Queen   - 'Live Killers'

Plus I got to listen to Whitesnake for the very first time on '**Ready an' Willing**' and it all went on from there.

I managed to see Whitesnake at the Cornwall Coliseum – one of my very first concerts (actually my second) and then another two times thereafter on subsequent tours. I then went on to catch them at Donington in '83 and New Year's Eve at Wembley Arena in '87. More recently I have seen them twice at Download Festival and once in Cardiff.

At one of the Download Festival's I also had the pleasure to see David Coverdale do a 'solo' Press Conference, which was a dream come true as he is very articulate and just such a likeable guy (I also attended a KISS press conference once at Download Festival, which was an amazing experience too).

From listening to them on cassette to purchasing their CD's and seeing them live, they have always been a very entertaining act in all of their incarnations – and there have been many over the years, with David staying the only constant throughout.

So, over this Book, we will look at the albums, the concerts and peoples opinions on the Band and David Coverdale, the 13th Book in the 'Fans Have Their Say' series of Books.

Ian Carroll
December 2019

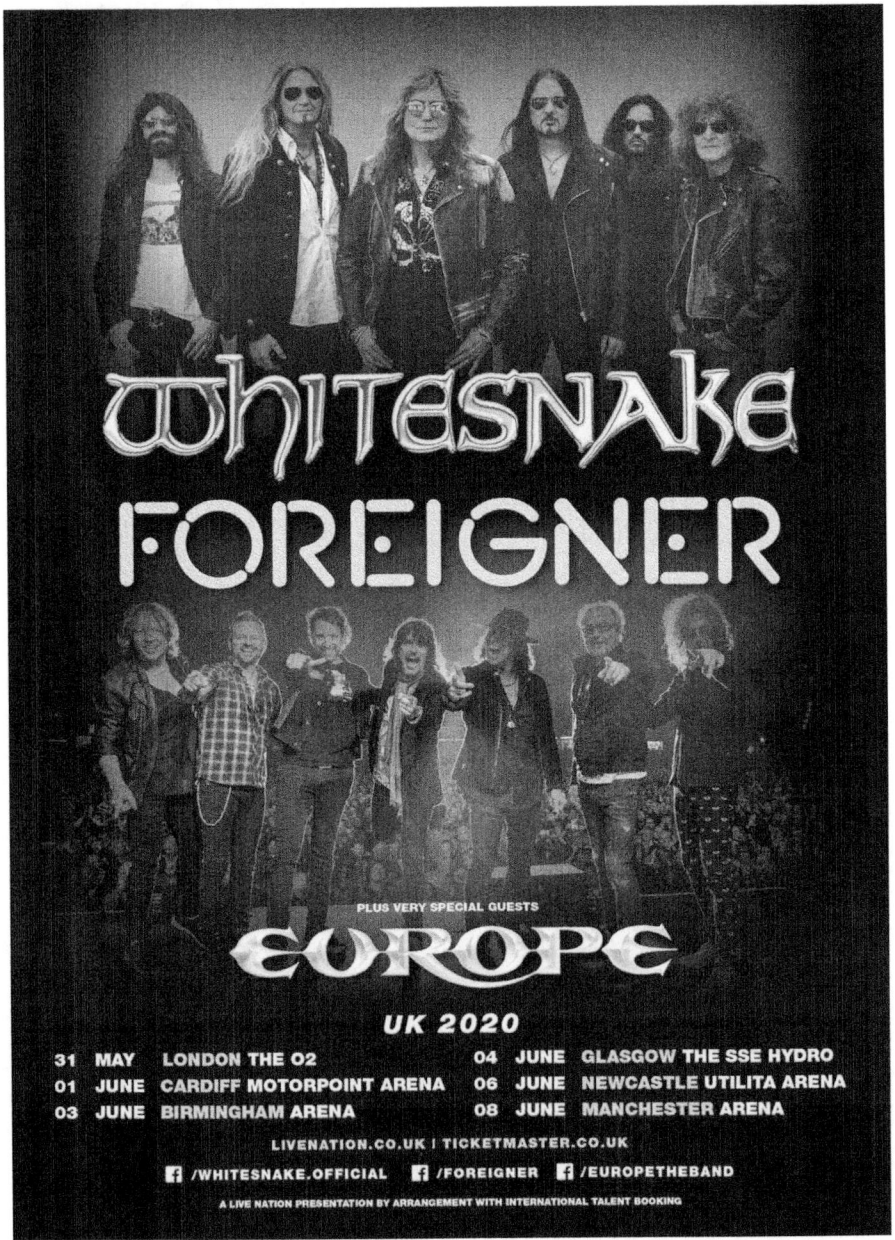

Trouble

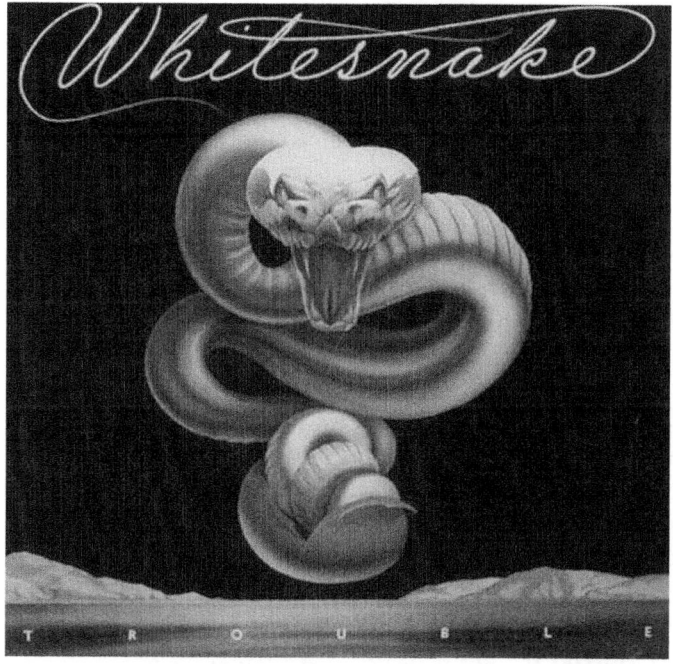

1) Take Me with You……………………..4:45
2) Love to Keep You Warm……………….3:44
3) Lie Down (A Modern Love Song)……...3:14
4) Day Tripper…………………………...3:47
5) Nighthawk (Vampire Blues)…………..3:39
6) The Time Is Right for Love……………3:26
7) Trouble………………………………..4:48
8) Belgian Tom's Hat Trick……………….3:26
9) Free Flight……………………………..4:06
10) Don't Mess with Me…………………..3:25

Release Date: October 1978
Producer: Martin Birch
Singles: 'Lie Down (A Modern Love Song)',
'The Time Is Right for Love / Come On'

"A true masterpiece, as the next four. For me the early years were simply the BEST."
Vík Hönö (Akureyri, Iceland)

"I first bought the album on release. The original white cover.
Had it painted on the back of my denim jacket, it looked amazing. It was the first gig I ever went to - Bristol Colston Hall, Magnum were supporting.
Saw Whitesnake on every tour until the hair metal version."
Tim Powell (Blaby, Leicestershire, UK)

"Absolutely love this album, been played to death on CD and vinyl."
Jason Haragan (Tenterden, Kent, UK)

*"Brilliant album, alongside the '**Snakebite**' e.p!"*
D.T. Gray (Scotland, UK)

*"First album I bought of Whitesnake was '**Lovehunter**', which then inspired me to buy '**Trouble**'.*
It remains as one of my favourite albums and the original artwork is far superior.
*A little known fact for you regarding '**Would I Lie To You**'. A friend and I gave David Coverdale a pin badge that said 'would I lie to you just to get in your pants'. What a great surprise we had when they released '**Come an' Get It**', and saw this track listed!*
David even mentioned us on a radio show as being the inspiration for this song."
Pauline Saunders (UK)

"The catalyst album for the start of a great band and for me the best line up."
Gary Clarke (UK)

"Brutal, exciting. The snake has poisoned me..."
Mar Gramon (Seville, Spain)

*"I love early Whitesnake, and '**Trouble**' was a solid start.*
*In my view the albums steadily improved from '**Lovehunter**' through to '**Ready an' Willing**' and then '**Come an' Get It**'.*
*Best of though was the live album, '**Live…in the Heart of the City**'. Whitesnake wasn't the same once the line up with Bernie split; although live with Mel Galley and Cozy Powell they were still great."*
Eddie Tee (Huddersfield, UK)

Whitesnake "Trouble"
0946 359688 2 8
Alternative Sleeve Artwork for Trouble LP

Whitesnake
TROUBLE

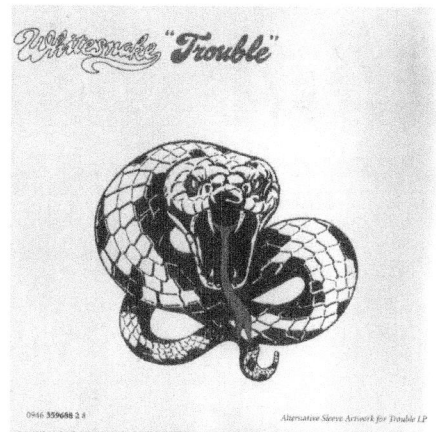

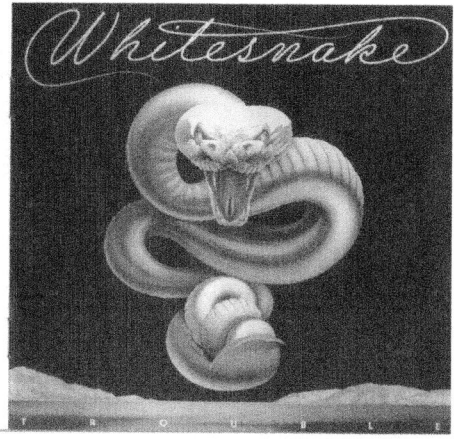

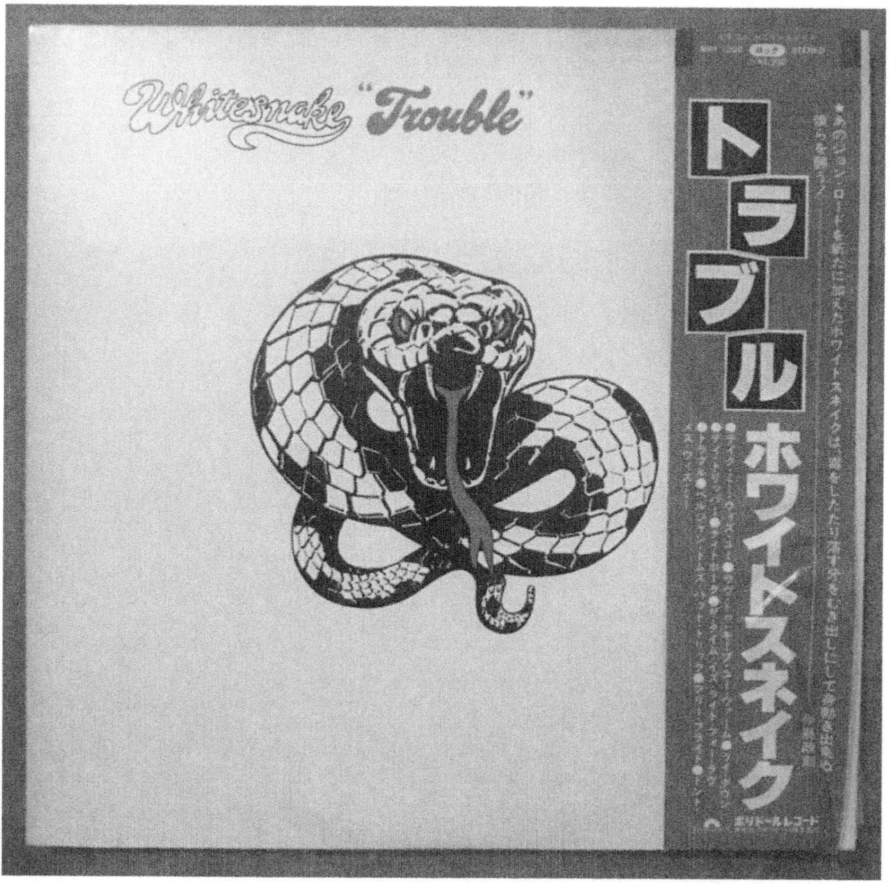
Whitesnake "Trouble"
トラブル
ホワイトスネイク

Argentina

(Including – 'My Favourite Whitesnake Concert')

"Whitesnake, I'm a fan from 1980 - 2019! The best!"
Eduardo Adrian Torres (Buenos Aires)

Lovehunter

1) Long Way from Home..........................4:58
2) Walking in the Shadow of the Blues..........4:26
3) Help Me Thro' the Day........................4:40
4) Medicine Man.................................4:00
5) You 'n' Me...................................3:25
6) Mean Business................................3:49
7) Love Hunter..................................5:38
8) Outlaw.......................................4:04
9) Rock 'n' Roll Women..........................4:44
10) We Wish You Well............................1:39

Release Date: 1st October 1979
Producer: Martin Birch
Singles: 'Long Way from Home'

"For some reason I am reminded of 'Smell the Glove'."
Jimmy Sparks (Texas, USA)

*"Love that album.
I had a big back patch on my denim cut-off in the early '80s, some liked it some didn't, lol.
Still have a tour program somewhere, one of my fave albums ever."*
Steve Whitehouse (Birmingham, UK)

*"One of their best...
Drew the front cover on a pair of jeans when I was 14, God knows what my parents must have thought..."*
Robert Vyse (Newcastle Under Lyme, UK)

*"My first Whitesnake album!
The album cover was enough of a selling point as any and the music did not disappoint! Overall an extremely solid album with loads of great songs but **'Rock 'n' Roll Women**' quickly became the favourite.
I had heard Whitesnake before, as this was just some 16-17 years ago, but I had no idea at the time that they used to be a bluesy hard rock act, before the more glamorous era of the mid '80s (which I honestly wasn't a fan of, so I would probably not have bought it if not for the album cover), so Whitesnake quickly became a favourite in my teens.
Here you also get the ultimate dynamics between Bernie Marsden and Mickey Moody. Most people say **'Ready an' Willing'** is the highlight of their collaboration, but I say that its definitely on **'Lovehunter'** - you hear those two players just having it out on each other!
I mean... **'You 'n' Me'**. The absolutely relentless slide guitar vs. Bernie's extremely vicious riffing on top, an extremely well written song with some of the best musicians that rock had to offer? They could never quite top that, in my opinion!"*
David Olofsson Harkonnen (Stockholm, Sweden)

*"Best Cover Art ever - first Whitesnake Album I bought - still have the vinyl version and twice on CD.
Title track - very tongue in cheek."*
Gary Clarke (UK)

The Fan Have Their Say #13 Whitesnake: In the Still of the Night...

"Not sure that cover would go down so well nowadays."
Peter Squires (Tripoli)

"Had the album and t-shirt."
Keith Holt (UK)

"Big one.
The 'real' Whitesnake in my opinion. Fucking rock, hard, heavy rock 'n' roll with a little blues"
Enrico Ravasio (In the World)

"My kinda 'Snake' - bluesy!"
Azlan Mohammed (In the World)

"My favourite album."
Vivienne Ben David (Yeruham, Israel)

13

The Fan Have Their Say #13 Whitesnake: In the Still of the Night...

"Certain countries, they had to put stickers over the naughty bits. I remember; I bought it in Germany."
Sean Scully (Ballymena, Northern Ireland, UK)

"Great album."
Gary Wallder (UK)

"No comment! The true golden Whitesnake years."
Vík Hönö (Akureyri, Iceland)

"This WAS Whitesnake.
*I lost interest in the band after the '**Slide It In**' album."*
Joe Azzopardi (In the World)

"I'm love hunter baybe..."
Vivienne Ben David (Yeruham, Israel)

"1979 was a good a good year for a thirteen year boy.
Blondie was a regular on Top of the Pops, 'Charlie's Angels' was on the TV and Linda Carter was playing 'Wonder Woman'.
Then there was the latest album cover from Whitesnake, '**Lovehunter**'! The cover depicted a naked woman about to be devoured by a mean looking serpent.
I had been Christmas shopping at Woolworth's in Wallsend with my eleven-year-old brother. We were looking for Rod Stewart's latest album for my Mam when we came across it. Remember back then there were no CD's, this was 12 inches of brilliant artwork and the effect it had on me was instant. I mentioned it to my friend at school the next day. He had heard the album and told me I should buy it.
"It's about time you stopped buying those football magazines," he told me.
At that time, in my wildest dreams, I was to play football for Newcastle United or Manchester City.
My brother and I clubbed our pocket money together and bought the album. Rod Stewart's 'Greatest Hits Vol 1' would have to wait. There was still forty-one shopping days to Christmas.
On the bus home I couldn't resist looking at the cover. I loved the Whitesnake logo, which I later realized was being used for the first time. On the back were pictures of the band. The singer had this fantastic head of hair. I couldn't wait to get back and play it.
When I arrived home Mary was there, she was a long standing friend of my mother's and she came once a week for her dinner and then would entertain us by reading our tea leaves in our empty cups.
When I showed my mother the album she couldn't believe it. Mary nearly fainted.
After careful inspection of the album to check there were no scratches I was allowed to play it. At that time all we had was an old gramophone, which could play 33-rpm records as well as 78's. A far cry from today where nearly every house is full of modern technology for playing music. The sound was a bit dodgy to say the least but the opening track, '**Long Way From Home**', sounded amazing. Next up was '**Walking in the Shadow of the Blues**'. This song just blew me away. Despite them saying it was a bit heavy I knew my Mam and Mary liked the music, usually they never stopped talking. Mary had even gone as far to read the lyrics on the inner sleeve.
"Have you read these words? 'Believe me when I say I would drink you dry...'"
The look of horror on her face was a picture,
"Oh my God and these songs '**Medicine Man**' and '**Lovehunter**', well I never."

Looking back now it was almost pure theatre. My Mam and Mary retired to the kitchen to dye each other's hair and no doubt converse in the loss of innocence of my brother and me.
We played the life out that album. By the time we went to bed my brother knew nearly all of the words. He loved to sing. We shared a room. In the dark waiting to go to sleep I asked him to sing '**Long Way from Home**', which he duly did. One thing was certain. I didn't want to be a footballer anymore; I wanted to be a rock star.
At school the next day I discussed the album with my friend, he introduced me to other bands and my love of rock music, and in particular Whitesnake, had begun.
I had never heard of David Coverdale, Whitesnake or of Deep Purple and although I didn't know it at that time, I was to start an incredible journey, a journey through birth, marriage and death that is still going on today.
Chris Handley (Newcastle upon Tyne)

Austria

(Including – 'My Favourite Whitesnake Concert')

"Donington Park 1990 with Steve Vai and Adrian Vandenberg."
Valeska Manarin (Klagenfurt)

"Donington 1981...all star line up.
'Ready an' Willing' just released, me on an Interrail tour on my way from Valencia Spain – incredible!!
Blackfoot discovery of that day. Local heroes Slade giving it all...
AC/DC's only European show in 1981.
38 yrs ago, still taking power and energy from that day. Still got my ticket in my homemade Purple shrine.
Keep on rocking from Graz Austria."
Hansjörg Sitner (Graz, Austria)

Ready an' Willing

1) Fool for Your Loving............4:17
2) Sweet Talker......................3:38
3) Ready an' Willing.................3:44
4) Carry Your Load..................4:06
5) Blindman.........................5:09
6) Ain't Gonna Cry No More........5:52
7) Love Man.........................5:04
8) Black and Blue...................4:06
9) She's a Woman...................4:07

Release Date: 31st May 1980
Producer: Martin Birch
Singles: 'Fool for Love Loving', 'Ready an' Willing', 'Sweet Talker/Ain't Gonna Cry No More'

"For me this album was the real Whitesnake, good old fashioned no nonsense blues rock.
There's some wonderful lyrics and songs on this album, I myself love '**Blindman**'.
But I also realise why David Coverdale had to change things up later on for the modern era of big hair and ballads.
But this album is great song writing and musicianship. One of my favourites."
Brian Richards (St. Austell, Cornwall, UK)

"'**Blindman**' for me, but absolutely love the whole album."
Jason Haragan (Tenterden, Kent, UK)

"'**Blindman**' - excellent track. Almost as good as the solo album!"
Stuart Bartlett (UK)

"I remember first hearing '**FFYL**' on the radio - couldn't wait for the LP to be released..."
Gilles Oberson (In the World)

"Sweet satisfaction..."
Vivienne Ben David (Yeruham, Israel)

"Mint album."
Andy Zack Gingle (Long Eaton, UK)

"Great Album from The Best line up Whitesnake ever had."
Alan Williams (UK)

"Great LP."
Robert Vyse (Newcastle Under Lyme, UK)

"I remember when I first bought this album. Saved up pocket money for three weeks to buy it.
A few years later '**Ain't Gonna Cry...**' was my singing audition to join my first band at college. To this day I love that song and I told Bernie so at a guitar show a few years back.
Timeless album.
Dave Collopy (UK)

"Still have it."
Jarlath Martin (Ballinderry, Northern Ireland, UK)

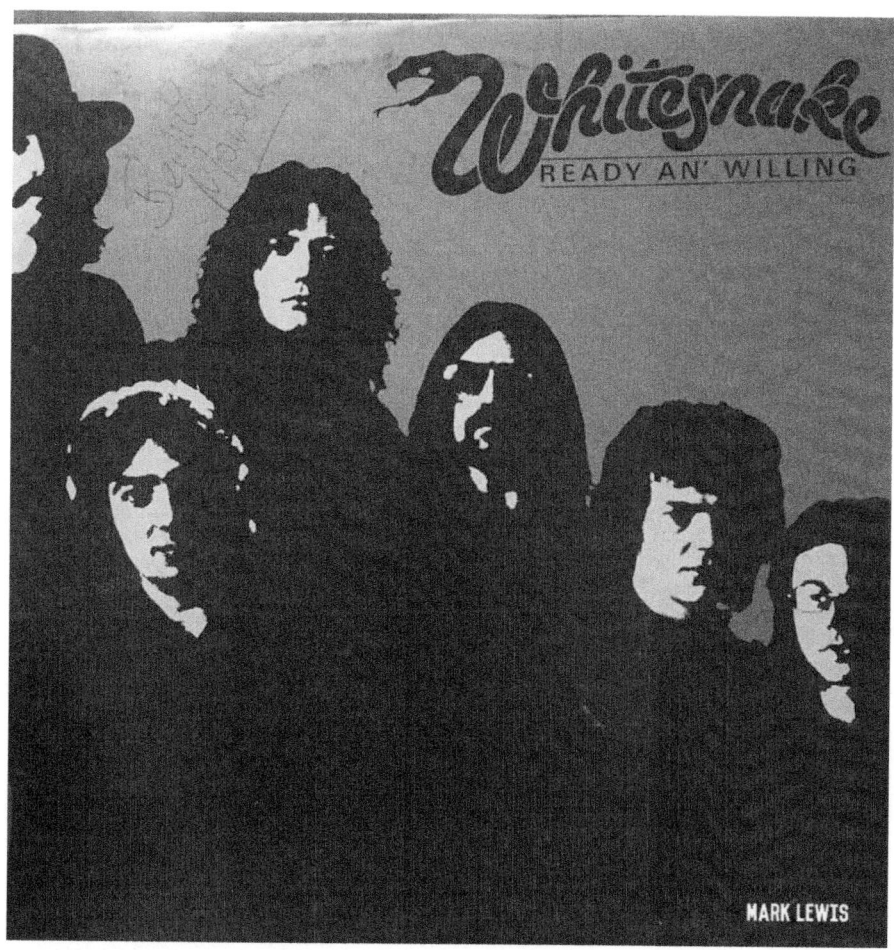

"My fav bluesnake."
Phil de Blois (In the World)

*"What a great album. Still have the program for that too lol.
I must have played every song off that when I was learning guitar.
Fond memories."*
Steve Whitehouse (Birmingham, UK)

"Great Album!!"
Barry Booth (Burntisland, Fife, Scotland, UK)

"Was 14 - a total game changer album."
Patrick Murray (UK)

"The 1st album with Ian Paice on drums and what a difference it made. For me, 'FFYL', 'R & W', 'Blindman', and 'Ain't Gonna Cry No More' are amongst the best tracks WS ever recorded.
The album is laden with soul and passion, and DC was at his peak around this time.
The original 'FFYL' encapsulates everything that was great about early WS in one song."
Kenny Mathers (Dundee, Scotland, UK)

"Excellent album."
Carlos Jaramillo Retemal (Punta Arenas, Chile)
"Who can forget 'Fool For Your Loving'. And what a solo!"
Andy Chambers (UK)

"Sweet satisfaction..."
Vivienne Ben David (Yeruham, Israel)

"Mint album."
Andy Zack Gingle (Long Eaton, UK)

"Great Album from The Best line up Whitesnake ever had."
Alan Williams (UK)

"Great LP."
Robert Vyse (Newcastle Under Lyme, UK)

"***Ain't Gonna Cry No More***' - *probably one of my top 5 Classic Whitesnake Tracks of all time."*
Gary Clarke (UK)

"As a long haired 17 year old way back in 1980 we waited for hours at the stage door of Sheffield City Hall to see our Gods.
The bus turned up and they let us on, only Bernie signed my album but that was enough. It's been treasured ever since.
Whitesnake were never the same, but 1980 was a mighty year, true rock and blues. Luv Ya Bernie!"
Mark Lewis (UK)

Best Whitesnake Album, best Whitesnake line-up."
Ian Evans (Aylesbury, Buckinghamshire, UK)
"I just played it tonight! Great album!"
Larry Mingus (Bellevue, Ohio, USA)

"Great xx."
Julie Blake Evans (Rhondda, Wales, UK)

"One of their best albums."
Rajeev Rana (Kathmandu, Nepal)

"My favorite."
Karin Welzel (Columbus, Ohio, USA)

The Fan Have Their Say #13 Whitesnake: In the Still of the Night...

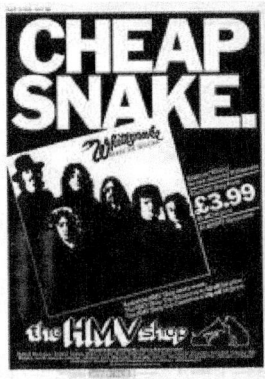

*"Loved Whitesnake since I saw them at Oxford on the '**Lovehunter**' tour. Bought '**Ready an' Willing**' the day it arrived at Disc Discounts in Bicester. The proprietor asked if I wanted it signed so I said yes please. He knew Bernie Marsden and a week later I swapped the cover for one signed by the band.*
I live in Melbourne Australia now and still have the album.
*One of their best. '**Carry Your Load**', '**Blindman**', '**Ain't Gonna Cry No More**' - great songs, great times."*
Mart Jaggs (Melbourne, Australia)

"This was one of the earliest albums that I ever had, on cassette! I remember the days when I used to play this on 'ghetto blaster' in our local park or at the railway station when we were 'supposed' to be trainspotting!!! (Actually writing down the numbers of the trains, not overdosing on heroin like the film...).
*I absolutely loved '**Fool For Your Loving**' and it was that one song initially that got me into the band and made me desperate to see them live – always waited for them to play it live on 'Top of the Pops', but I think at the time there was a strike at the BBC and 'TOTP' was cancelled and so they never got to play. Also, really like the tracks '**Ain't Gonna Cry No More**' and '**Ready an' Willing**'.*
I also had a huge poster advertising the album on my bedroom wall, which I had obtained from a nearby record shop when they were having a clear-out."
Ian Carroll (Plymouth, Devon, UK)

"Ready and Waiting!"
Angel Vincente Peñaranda (Spain)

The Fan Have Their Say #13 Whitesnake: In the Still of the Night...

Bahrain

(Including – 'My Favourite Whitesnake Concert')

"I discovered Whitesnake in 1981 and to this day they have remained my favorite band.
The original spirit of the band 'died' in 1983 when Sykes and Powell brought a much more heavier sound. Until 1983, Coverdale was arguably the greatest blues-rock singer ever. In Neil Murray they had an exceptional musician whose bass lines gave a lot of depth to their music. The early years produced exceptional music - blending rock, blues and soul in a unique package. Superb songwriting, cheeky lyrics and outstanding performances were the norm.
The music was fun and warm. It was an invitation to have fun.
Once Sykes joined, the blues took a backseat and the heart and soul of the band got lost. Whitesnake became a different animal.
Commercially extremely successful but artistically nowhere near as original and fulfilling.
The voice, the look, the sound changed - which is not an issue per se - and turned a very soulful band with a unique personality into a hard rock band that looked - and to a certain extent- sounded like a lot of their competitors.
To me the early years will always remain special. Nostalgia is part of it as I grow older, but it is the sheer passion and the exceptional quality of the songs that will always make me love this band more than any others.
Laurent Biehly (Manama, Bahrain)

Live…in the Heart of the City

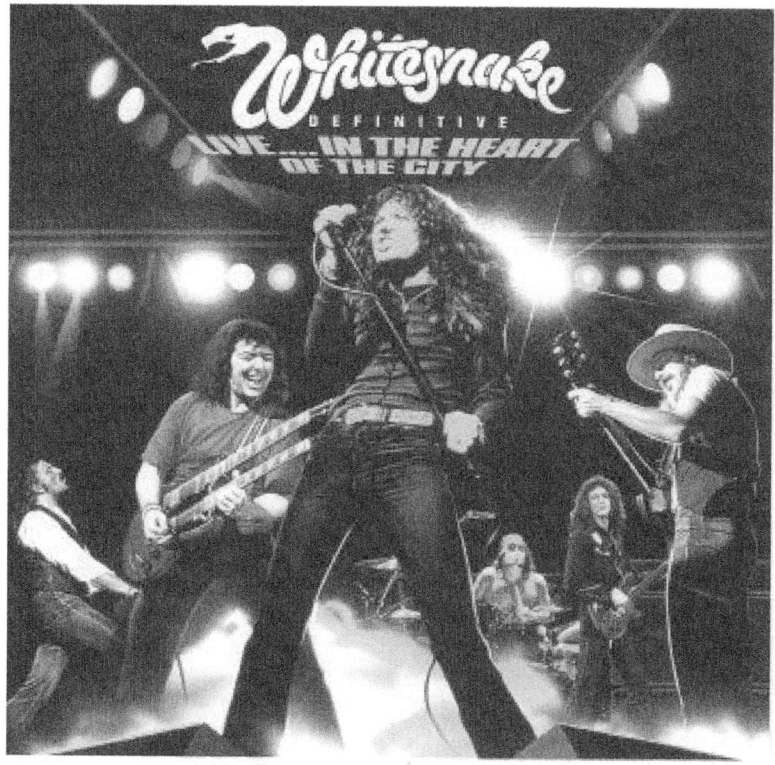

1) Come On……………………………….3:38
2) Sweet Talker………………………….. 4:16
3) Walking in the Shadow of the Blues………5:00
4) Love Hunter……………………………10:41
5) Fool for Your Loving………………………4:58
6) Ain't Gonna Cry No More…………………6:21
7) Ready an' Willing……………………….4:46
8) Take Me with You……………………...6:28
9) Come On……………………………….3:32
10) Might Just Take Your Life…………………4:55
11) Lie Down……………………………….3:33
12) Ain't No Love in the Heart of the City………6:38
13) Trouble………………………………….4:56
14) Mistreated……………………………...10:40

Release Date: 3rd November 1980
Producer: Martin Birch
Singles: 'Ain't No Love in the Heart of the City'

"One of the best live albums!!!"
Rajeev Rana (Kathmandu, Nepal)

"One of the best Live Albums ever - I actually queued at my local record shop to open to get this and got it fresh from the box - they had not even unpacked them for display.
"Let me fucking hear you."
Gary Clarke (UK)

"Great."
Thomas Ruffing (Furpach, Germany)

"We saw this line-up 7 times between '79 and '81 - put this album on and close your eyes, it's just like being there. A fantastic live band."
Mark Lewis (UK)

"I have this album on, vinyl, cassette, CD and download!
My absolute favourite live album."
Joe Azzopardi (In the World)

"Up there with the greats, Deep Purple 'Made In Japan', Schenker 'One Night in Budokan'."
Best Whitesnake line up."
Adrian Woods (Maidstone, Kent)

"Great album. Actually bought it on Japanese import as well.
Had an awesome cover."
Andy Chambers (UK)

"Holy crap, 39 years! Lol.
This album got played to death, and I'm not big on live albums either. Awesome."
Steve Whitehouse (Birmingham, UK)

"I have the 2 LP version and a single vinyl version."
Phil de Blois (In the World)

"One of my favorites!!"
Jack Kranz (Santa Fe, Tennessee, USA)

"One of the finest live albums ever released, this is THE Whitesnake!"
Chris Beddall (Moira, Derby, UK)

"Underrated live album(S)... Should release the full show imo...???"
Shaun Maher (Liverpool, UK)

"Best line up ever."
Billy Maddison (Bishop Aukland, UK)

*"A fantastic album and a great representation of the band, as they were. Never get sick of playing it and have given it a spin this afternoon.
5 stars"*
Michael Denney (UK)

"Good representation of this line-up My personal favorite."
Rusty Lewis-LeMaster (Bloomington, Indiana, USA)

"Still got it."
Ian Spencer (Poole, Dorset, UK)

"Best live album there is."
Per Jensen (Norrköping, Sweden)

"One of the best live ALBUMS ever recorded."
Paul Clarke (Nantwich, UK)

"The first time I saw Whitesnake live was at Donington in 1983, after which I immediately went out and purchased this double LP.
I just wanted to be able to experience that 'livesnake' buzz again and again. It didn't disappoint and it is still a favourite driving album... and obviously cranked up to 11... Come On!!"
Paul Hollingworth (UK)

"Sing for me London..."
Paul Donnelly (Consett, UK)

"One of the best album covers."
Joe Vetrone (St. Louis, USA)

"Super album of a great time for WS."
Ale G. Gabanatto (Mogliano Veneto, Italy)

"Gr8 bluesy 'Snake!"
Azlan Mohammed (Trinidad & Tobago)

"I remember watching Whitesnake at Reading Festival bank holiday weekend 1980, they were the very last act to play that weekend.
David Coverdale announced the live album was coming out at the end of the year, I remember he also announced it was a **ther******.
First time I remember hearing that horrible word."
Raymond Dixon (Carlisle, Cumbria, UK)

"I love this album! One of the best live LP's."
Leon Kogan (St. Petersburg, Russia)

"One of my All-time favourite live albums.
Bought it the first time on Vinyl in 1980 on the Day of Release.
Since then several Times more: single CD, Japanese Card box CD, re-mastered Double CD and finally as Reissue 180g Double vinyl.
Still Whitesnake's best live album (and I collected some over the last 40 Years). Great Versions of classic timeless songs."
Reinhard Arand (Germany)

"Love it."
Norine Wolff (Clearwater, Florida, USA)

*"**Ain't No Love In The Heart Of The City**' must have been the anthem of the '80s for a lot of people. It certainly was for myself and my friends. You could see how moved David was at every gig when the audience out sung him. And, what better use was there for the poster than to stick it on the bedroom wall and cover up the gaudy wallpaper of the '80s!"*
Pauline Saunders (UK)

"My first double album! I bought it in 1985."
Carlos Fernando Leser (Montenegro, Brazil)

"The real Whitesnake!"
Alfeu Dante (In the World)

"I have this record on vinyl... I gave it to my Chinese soul who takes care of me from heaven today!
We met in 1987 and the album that of '87 never separated ... 23 years together ... love, love and love this band x forever!"
Sonia Varesse (Córdoba, Argentina)

"One of the best ever live albums!"
DT Gray (Scotland, UK)

"My Dad gave me a copy of this when I was around 13 –
"See what you think to that" he said.
Hooked from that day on."
Paul Whitehead (Leeds, UK)

"Think I got mine from HMV in Church St. Paid like sumthin' daft like £2.99... great days."
Shaun Maher (Liverpool, UK)

Brazil

(Including – 'My Favourite Whitesnake Concert')

"I went to the 'Rock in Rio' show 2019 - for me was the best show. Many people were crying and singing together, was F.. awesome."
Rodrigo Jack (Rio de Janeiro)

Rock in Rio
Parque Olímpico, Rio de Janeiro
28th September 2019

Bad Boys
Slide It In
Love Ain't No Stranger
Hey You (You Make Me Rock)
Slow an' Easy
Trouble Is Your Middle Name
Is This Love
Here I Go Again
Still of the Night
Burn

The Fan Have Their Say #13 Whitesnake: In the Still of the Night...

Come an' Get It

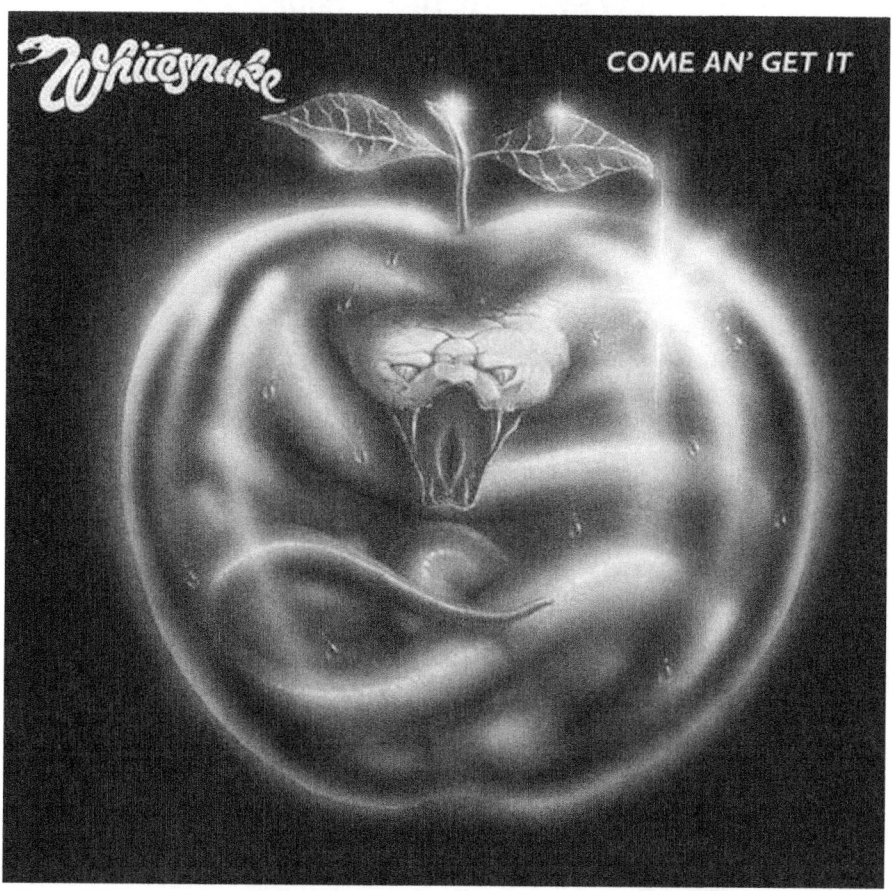

1) Come an' Get It……………………...3:59
2) Hot Stuff…………………………….3:22
3) Don't Break My Heart Again………..4:03
4) Lonely Days, Lonely Nights………..4:16
5) Wine, Women an' Song…………….3:45
6) Child of Babylon…………………...4:48
7) Would I Lie to You………………...4:29
8) Girl………………………………….3:55
9) Hit an' Run………………………….3:23
10) Till the Day I Die…………………..4:23

Release Date: 11th April 1981
Producer: Martin Birch
Singles: 'Don't Break My Heart Again', 'Would I Lie to You'

"Talk box, bluesy, killer riffs. My favorite Whitesnake album!"
Brian McNeill (Elon, North Carolina, USA)

"Epic Masterpiece!"
Ricardo Bailey (Port Of Spain, Trinidad and Tobago)

"Hello from Australia & a massive Whitesnake fan!
Particularly the early years!
I've loved 'em since I heard the ***Come an' Get It*** *album & the original live album in one beautiful stoned afternoon way back in about 1981.*
I've loved 'em ever since!
Cheers from the 'Land of Oz', that magical little land down under!"
Brett Peters (Australia)

"Love this album; Mickey Moody and Bernie Marsden were a great team."
Philip Ballard (Ridgeland, Mississippi, USA)

"The best Whitesnake album in my opinion! With the coolest cover art! Pure R&R from beginning to end! Never grow tired of this one!"
Andi Gatelangs Roxx (Trondheim, Norway)

"Loved this Album - not a poor track on. The Cover Art is sublime."
Gary Clarke (UK)

"Was my favourite album when it came out and still is. Haven't found anything to beat it yet. Clever how they got the tongue past the censors too."
Andy Chambers (UK)

"Curiously this album was difficult to obtain only a couple of years later. Picked up a copy from Roxcene records in Newport eventually sometime in 1984 - I think?"
Dave Smith Price (Frome, Somerset, UK)

5th of June 1981, Polygon Hotel, Southampton. (Sadly, no longer there...) David Coverdale kindly modelling our **'Come an' Get It'** *Snoopy apron. The greatest luck ever for my friends and I because we found out that Whitesnake weren't staying at their usual hotel and were booked in to the Polygon after their gig at The Gaumont.*

Eight of us in the bar with David until 4am, smoking Marlboro's, drinking copious amounts of brandy and Coke and chatting. Brief appearances from Micky and Bernie.

Milk train back to Eastleigh followed by a two-mile walk home!!"
Pauline Saunders (UK)

"My favorite Whitesnake album."
Martin Bradbury (Huyton, UK)

"I was sixteen when I bought this album."
Ale G. Gabonotto (Mogliano Veneto, Italy)

"First tour I saw Whitesnake at Staff's Bingley hall with Billy Squire supporting.
Pissed down all day and I was in the queue from about midday to get a good view, didn't put me off.
I've been a fan ever since and can't remember how many times I've seen DC live , met him once it was an honour , God bless em all.
Keith Rosten (Birmingham, UK)

"My favorite Whitesnake album!"
Carlos Pereira (Brazil)

"Use to listen to the singles that were on juke boxes in the UK, #TheVine #GtBardfield."
Peter Morris (Ngaruawahia, New Zealand)

"Love it."
Norine Wolff (Clearwater, Florida, USA)

"Watching an episode of the old TV series 'Minder' and this picture is on a Whitesnake poster on Terry's living room wall - and as a bonus, Suzy Quatro is in the episode too (acting, not singing sadly!!)."
Maureen Smith (Daventry, UK)

"Love it... saw them on that tour, Bingley Hall."
Robert Vyse (Newcastle Under Lyme, UK)

"Probably the most perfect album with the so-called classic WS line-up. That goes from song writing over Martin Birch's production to the fantastic cover artwork. **Fool For Your Loving**
Even if **'Don't Break My Heart Again'** *was not as successful as* **'Fool For Your Loving'** *before, it was a badass rocker!*
The epic **'Child of Babylon'** *was unique and incomparable to anything they had released before.*
The album clearly confirmed how important Bernie Marsden was as a songwriter and fine guitarist in this band."
Kwizatz Haderach (In the World)

"Superb album."
Andy Zack Gingle (Long Eaton, UK)

"Last album the classic Whitesnake line up toured to promote."
Raymond Dixon (Carlisle, Cumbria, UK)

"Their best work. Neil Murray said that too."
Mark Stevens (In the World)

"THE BEST 1."
Albert Schembri (Luqa, Malta)

*"This is the finest Whitesnake album that was ever released.
Really quality writing and in my humble opinion the height of creativity of the real band and not the sadly lacking later versions.
Neil Murray is mighty on the bass, Messrs Moody and Marsden have amazing synchronicity on the guitars, Jon Lord weaves magic with his Hammond, Ian Paice thunders and swings bring it all together on the drums, while David Coverdale groans and growls his heartfelt vocals topping off what is a legendary album.
For me 'Child of Babylon' is a highlight!"*
Aly Page (Sydney, Australia)

"Their best. The drum sound is incredible on this one. Great songs, terrific musicians."
Robert van Eedenburg (Apeldoorn, Netherlands)

"Brilliant album from when Whitesnake were a proper rock band."
Kev Arnold (Nottingham, UK)

"No comment! ... a true MASTERPIECE!!!"
Vík Hönö (Akureyri, Iceland)

"Priceless."
Sean Dixon (Aurora, Colorado, USA)

*"And of course the track that was the 10 minute encore at Donington later in '81, 'Wine, Women and Song'.
Saw them at the Hammy Odeon on 9th June 1981, touring this album. Excellent concert, and Jon Lord's birthday as well."*
Brian M. Chapple (In the World)

"A great album."
Jesús Buendía (Benalmádena, Spain)

"Thought I had died."
Debra Phillips (UK)

"Possibly my fave 'snake album…!!!"
Shaun Maher (Liverpool, UK)

Canada

(Including – 'My Favourite Whitesnake Concert')

"Rama, Ontario Canada a few years ago, front row VIP floors...awesome concert."
Mike Schmidt (Canada)

Casino Rama, Orillia, Ontario 18th June 2016

Bad Boys
Slide It In
Love Ain't No Stranger
The Deeper the Love
Fool for Your Loving
Sailing Ships / Judgement Day
Slow an' Easy
Crying in the Rain
Is This Love
Give Me All Your Love
Here I Go Again
Still of the Night

"My favorite band ever."
Lora Di Mora (Montreal)

Saints & Sinners

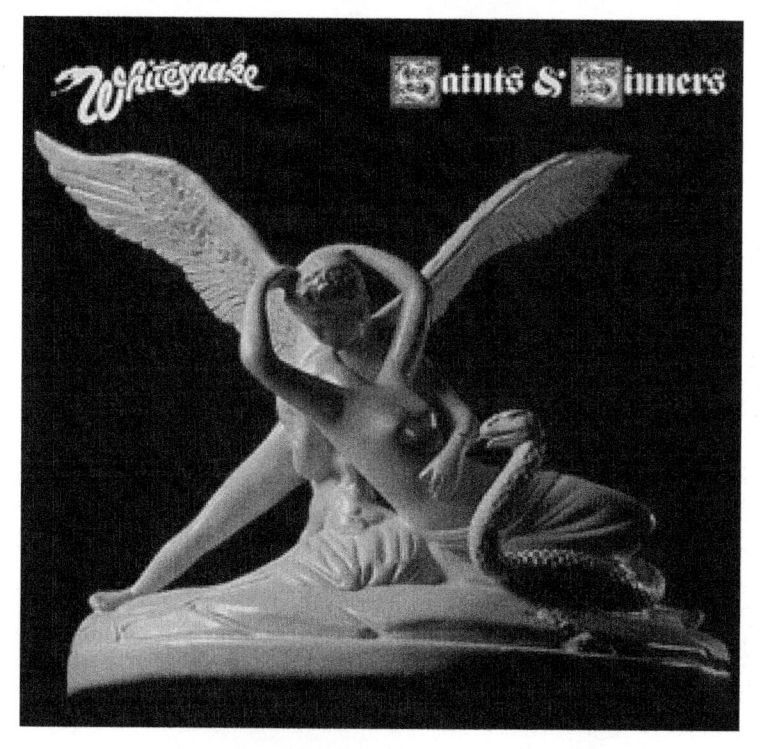

1) Young Blood......................3:30
2) Rough an' Ready.................2:52
3) Bloody Luxury...................3:23
4) Victim of Love..................3:33
5) Crying in the Rain..............6:00
6) Here I Go Again.................5:08
7) Love an' Affection..............3:09
8) Rock an' Roll Angels............4:07
9) Dancing Girls...................3:10
10) Saints an' Sinners.............4:25

Release Date: 25th November 1982
Producer: Martin Birch
Singles: 'Here I Go Again', 'Victim of Love'

"The album I never knew who played on it - Bernie or Mel, Cozy or Ian..."
Gilles Oberson (In the World)

"This tour!! Gutted I never bought a t-shirt..."
Jonathan Shaw (UK)

"**Crying in the Rain**' best track on the album for me."
Andy Chambers (UK)

"I love the album and all the ones before.
Seeing them in concert is the best feeling. It's like I'm 16 again! When they come out on stage it's like Wow!
I recently saw them in Melbourne, Florida. David has such a stage presence and I love how he dresses.
The passion the whole band has on stage keeps my youth alive a heart! Keep rocking!"
Kimberly Franks (Cocoa Beach, Florida, USA)

"Do like this album..."
Shaun Maher (Liverpool, UK)

"Great songs, love the album."
Rajeev Rana (Kathmandu, Nepal)

"Best album ever IMHO. Always been my fave Whitesnake album since I first bought it in the early '80s."
Martin Beames (UK)

"Wonderful.'
Mar Gramon (Seville, Spain)

"My 1st and best album, love it."
David Seddon (Atherton, Wigan, UK)

"A masterpiece. Forever."
Rick B. Miller (In the World)

"Schoolgirl memories."
Debra J. Phillips (UK)

The Fan Have Their Say #13 Whitesnake: In the Still of the Night...

FABIO MARIN

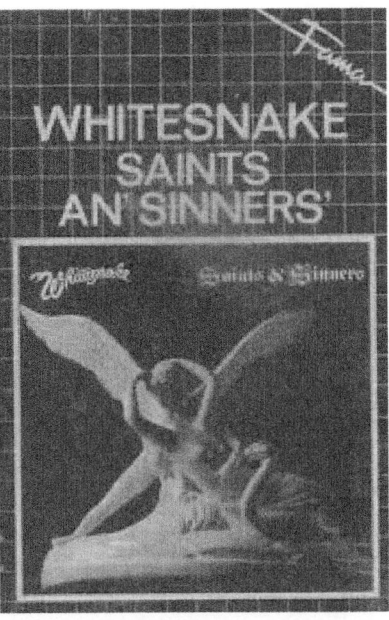

The Fan Have Their Say #13 Whitesnake: In the Still of the Night...

Chile

(Including – 'My Favourite Whitesnake Concert')

"Monster of Rock 2011, Movistar Arena, Chile."
Pablo Rivera (Chile)

Movistar Arena, Santiago, Chile, 20th September 2011

Best Years
Give Me All Your Love
Love Ain't No Stranger
Is This Love
Steal Your Heart Away
Forevermore
Love Will Set You Free
Here I Go Again
Still of the Night
Soldier of Fortune
Burn/Stormbringer

Slide It In

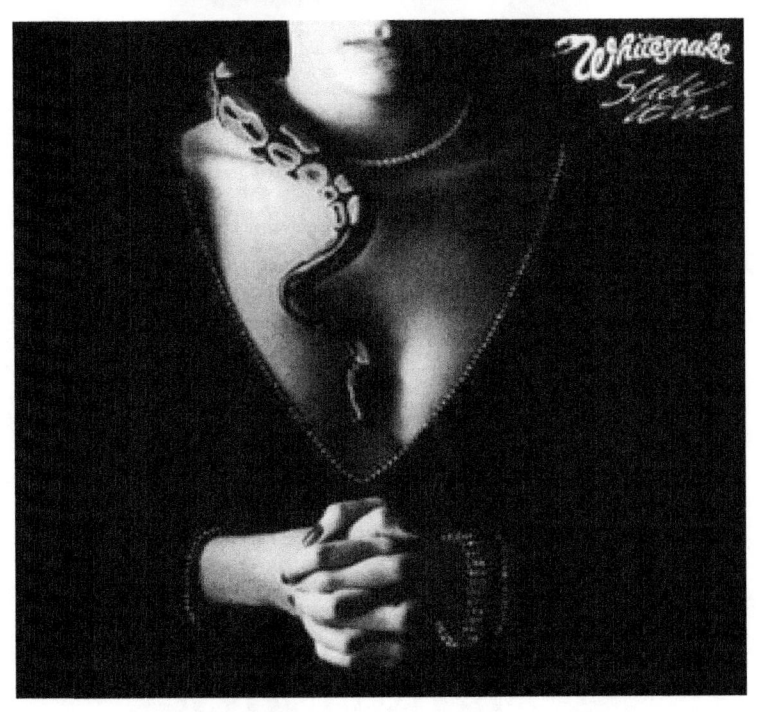

1) Gambler……………………3:57
2) Slide It In…………………..3:20
3) Standing in the Shadow………..3:32
4) Give Me More Time……………3:41
5) Love Ain't No Stranger…………4:13
6) Slow an' Easy………………..6:09
7) Spit It Out……………………4:11
8) All or Nothing………………..3:34
9) Hungry for Love……………….3:57
10) Guilty of Love………………..3:18

Release Date: 30th January 1984
Producer: Martin Birch
Singles: 'Guilty of Love', ' Give Me More Time',
             'Love Ain't No Stranger', 'Slow an' Easy'

"Great album."
Philip Krod Mende (Wrightstown, New Jersey, USA)

"Snakes heaviest album imo... US remix just nails it???"
Shaun Maher (Liverpool, UK)

*"**Slow an' Easy**' kicked ass."*
David Ilse (Barrington, Nova Scotia, Canada)

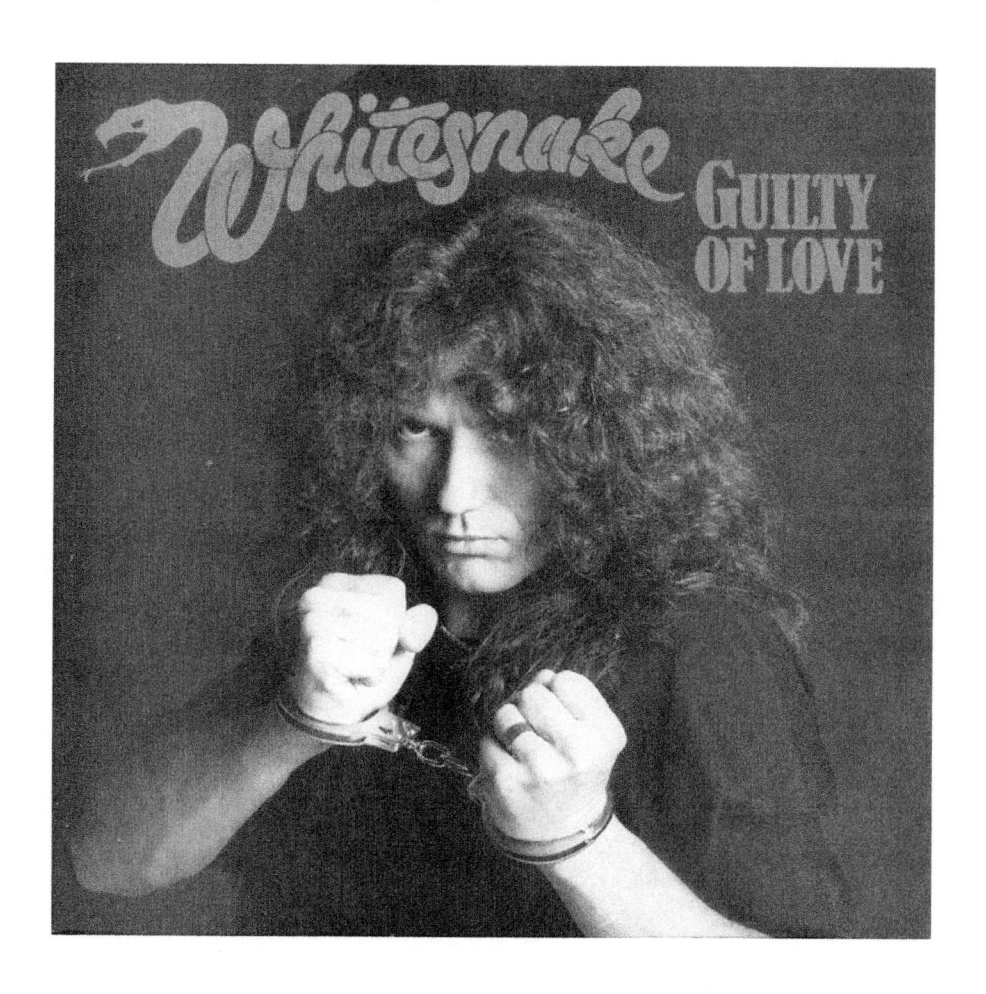

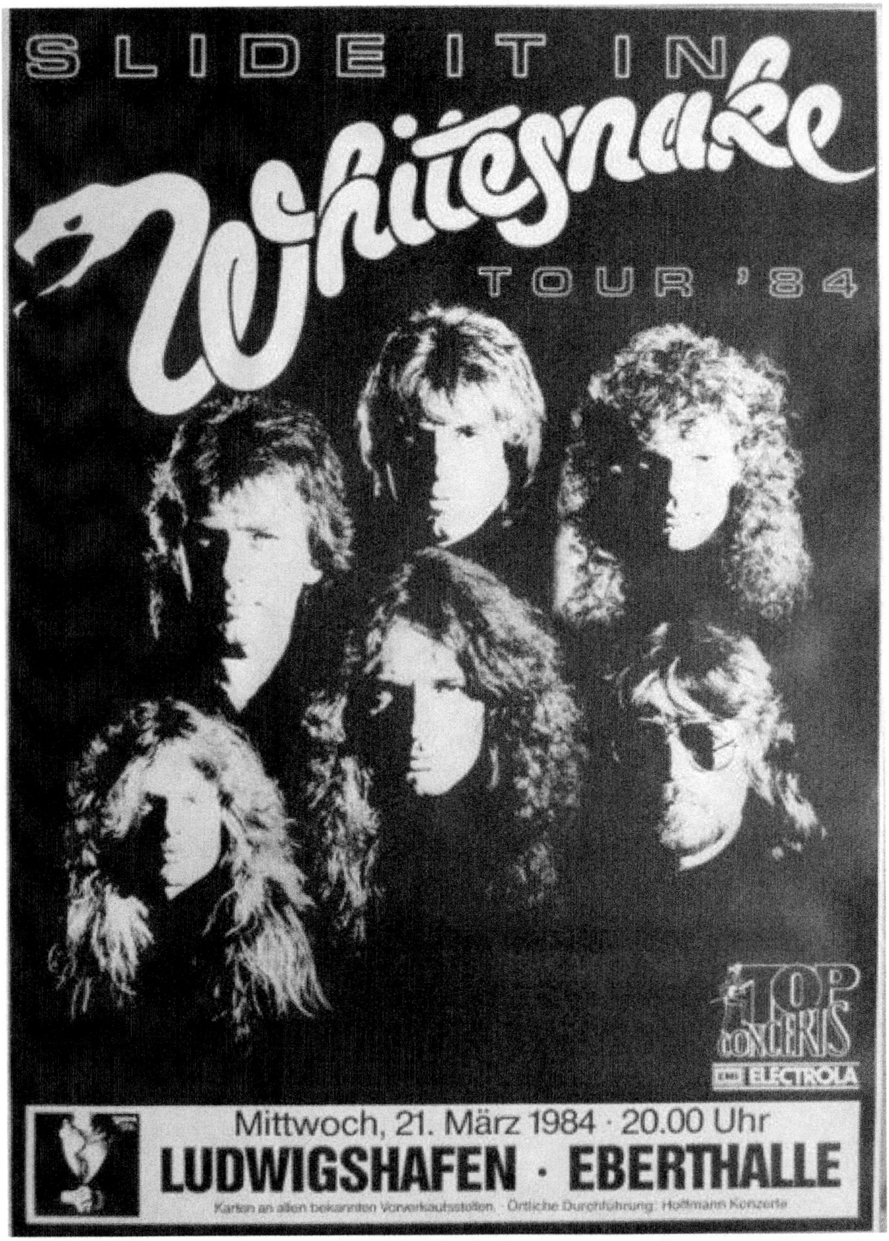
SLIDE IT IN
Whitesnake
TOUR '84
TOP CONCERTS
ELECTROLA
Mittwoch, 21. März 1984 · 20.00 Uhr
LUDWIGSHAFEN · EBERTHALLE

The Fan Have Their Say #13 Whitesnake: In the Still of the Night...

Germany

(Including – 'My Favourite Whitesnake Concert')

"My Favourite Show was San Antonio, April 17th. At the 3rd Song I became a real 'Whitesnakefan'.
I like his stage presence.
My favourite Whitesnake song is **'Still of the Night'**.
I am looking forward to seeing them in Munich, Hamburg and Dortmund."
Reading Eagle (Germany)

"Mannheim, Rosengarten 02.05.1981... hot and electric... as good as it gets!"
Hartmut Kreckel (Germany)

"Mannheim, Rosengarten May 1981."
Harmut Kreckel (Germany)

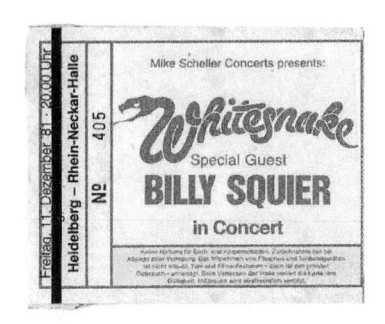

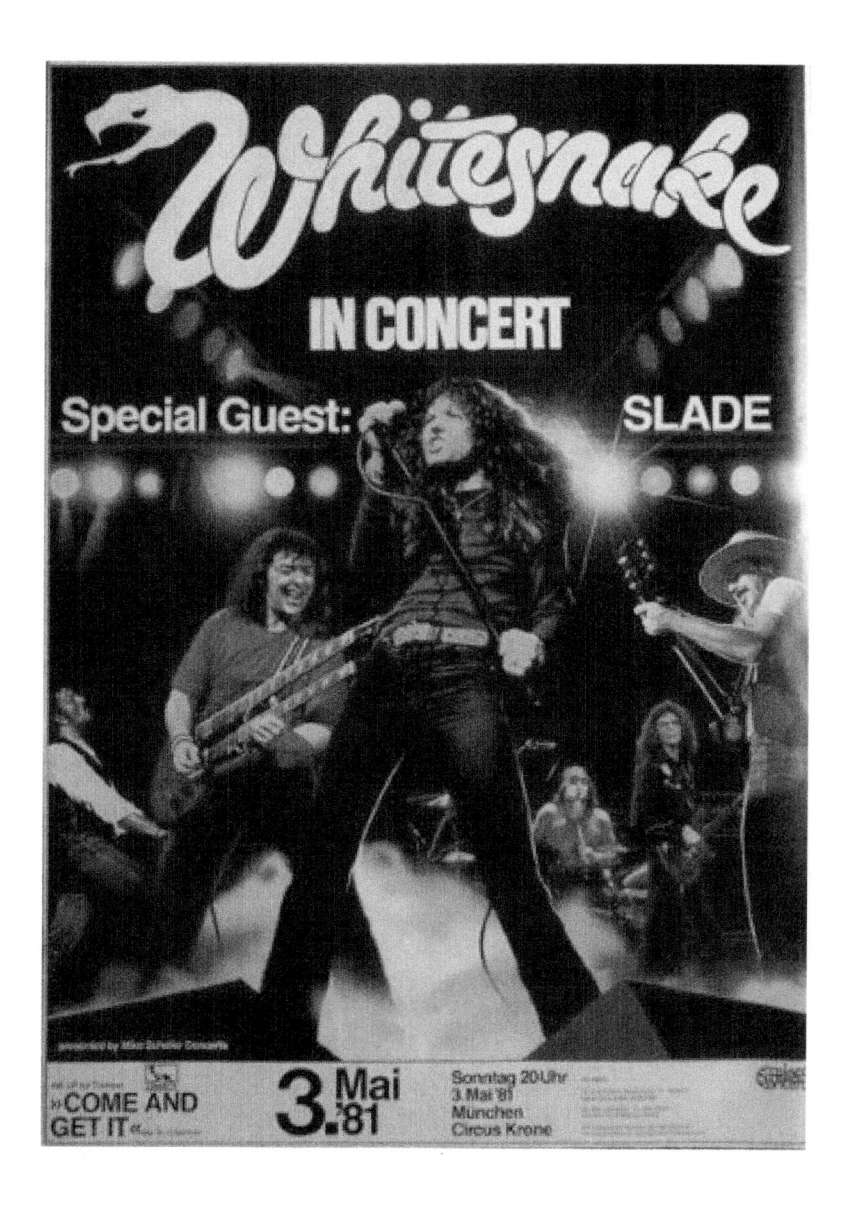

"08.26.1990 Utrecht Netherlands, homecoming concert of Adrian Vandenberg at 'Monsters of Rock'."
Arthur ter Avest (Flensburg)

"Nuremberg 1983."
Chris Mueller (Germany)

Whitesnake (1987)

1) Crying in the Rain '87..........5:37
2) Bad Boys.........................4:09
3) Still of the Night................6:38
4) Here I Go Again '87.............4:33
5) Give Me All Your Love..........3:30
6) Is This Love.....................4:43
7) Children of the Night...........4:24
8) Straight for the Heart..........3:40
9) Don't Turn Away................5:11

Release Date: 7th April 1987
Producer: Mike Stone / Keith Olsen
Singles: 'Still of the Night', ' Crying in the Rain', 'Here I Go Again '87', 'Is This Love', 'Give Me All Your Love'

"Top 3 hard rock albums of the '80s.
Full band and Coverdale was joined by a Sykes. What did he compose?
70% of the music on the album.
*'**Still of the Night**' - It sums it up."*
Urrizaga Fernando Ariel (Argentina)

"Listening to them now, WS is just AWESOME."
Philip Krod Mende (Wrightstown, New Jersey, USA)

"Timeless Masterpiece!"
Azlan Mohammed (Trinidad and Tobago)

"I was 16 when this album was released.
I had listened to Whitesnake's earlier work and liked it. I bought this and it was like WOW!
*John Sykes opening to '**Still of the Night**' and Coverdale's immense vocal power just amazed me. David was told he needed a guitar hero and he certainly found it in John.*
This album had such a strong influence on me and I still love it now."
Paul Whitehead (Leeds, UK)

"Great album."
Danijel Vincetić (Vijevo, Croatia)

"One of the best albums I ever heard.
*The singles '**Is This Love**' and '**Here I Go Again**' were on the radio here in the Netherlands in 1987. I loved it and bought the album a couple of months after it came out.*
Still one of my favorites.
I don't listen it too often anymore, because after a year or two, I am surprised that I forgot how good that album is. Great songs, not too soft and not too loud, so I can dream away while listening to the album.
(I bought the album on LP in 1987 or begin 1988 and later, in 2012, on CD)."
Richard Van Der Niet (Katwijk aan Zee, Netherlands)

"Iconiccccccc."
Nils Lips (IJmuiden, Netherlands)

"I became a fan because of the album 'Stormbringer' by Deep Purple. On this album there's a song 'Soldier of Fortune' of which I found a great video on YouTube from 1987 'To Tokyo Unplugged' by David Coverdale and Dutch Pride Adrian VandenBerg, guitarist.
That's when my love for Whitesnake started."
Treeske Soentken (Netherlands)

"The best."
Kurt Lahiff (Terranora, New South Wales, Australia)

The Fan Have Their Say #13 Whitesnake: In the Still of the Night...

The Fan Have Their Say #13 Whitesnake: In the Still of the Night...

Italy

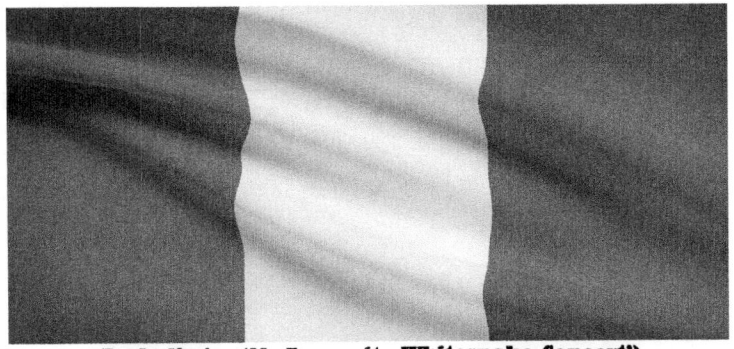

(Including – 'My Favourite Whitesnake Concert')

"Monsters of Rock' 1990."
Pasquale Iavarone (Siena, Italy)

Monsters of Rock Arena Parco Nord, Bologna, 30th August 1990

Slip of the Tongue
Slide It In
Judgement Day
Slow an' Easy
Kittens Got Claws
Adagio for Strato
Flying Dutchman Boogie
Is This Love
Cheap an' Nasty
Crying in the Rain
Fool For Your Loving
For the Love of God
The Audience is Listening
Here I Go Again
Bad Boys
Ain't No Love in the Heart of the City
Soldier of Fortune
Still of the Night

The Fan Have Their Say #13 Whitesnake: In the Still of the Night...

Slip of the Tongue

1) Slip of the Tongue..................5:20
2) Cheap an' Nasty....................3:28
3) Fool For Your Loving '89...........4:10
4) Now You're Gone...................4:11
5) Kittens Got Claws..................5:00
6) Wings of the Storm................5:00
7) The Deeper the Love..............4:22
8) Judgement Day....................5:15
9) Slow Poke Music..................3:59
10) Sailing Ships......................6:02

Release Date: 7th November 1989
Producer: Mike Clink / Keith Olsen
Singles: 'Judgement Day', 'Fool For Your Loving '89', 'The Deep the Love', 'Now You're Gone'

"Thank you, so beautiful."
Petra Leban (In the World)

"This album is not good."
Andy Iwanski (USA)

"I call this the guitar 'wars' SNAKE' - Vai and Vandenberg really 'squared off' on this album, killer timeless 'shred'!!"
Azlan Mohammed (Trinidad and Tobago)

*"30 yrs back the only Whitesnake song that I had listened to was '**Here I Go Again**'. And that was the very reason why I wanted to try out '**Slip of the Tongue**'.*
In my teens and heavily into metal, like anyone else I too was into Zep, Sabbath, Deep Purple, Priest, Maiden 'n' the likes. And my taking a chance turned out to be a delightful experience.
*The version of '**Fool For Your Loving**', '**Deeper the Love**' etc. turned me into a Coverdale fan.*
Though I haven't caught up with the entire discography, this one album, I reckon, as a must in a metalhead's collection."
Rajesh Parekat (Thrissur, India)

"Good album!"
Simon Zinach (Plains, Pennsylvania, USA)

I have the cassette, 'Slip of Tongue', 'Slide It In'. Baby..."
Charles Ngamlai (Umrongso, India)

"Great album."
Jonathon Shucha (Dahlonega, Georgia, USA)

Restless Heart

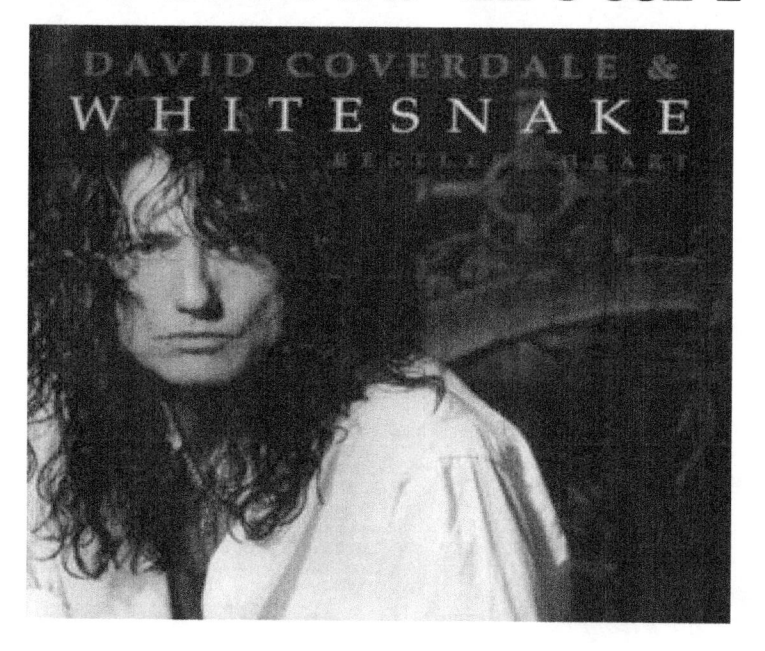

1) Don't Fade Away..................5:02
2) All in the Name of Love..........4:42
3) Restless Heart....................4:50
4) Too Many Tears....................5:44
5) Crying............................5:34
6) Stay With Me.....................4:09
7) Can't Go On......................4:27
8) You're So Fine...................5:10
9) Your Precious Love...............4:34
10) Take Me Back Again..............6:02
11) Woman Trouble Blues.............5:35

Release Date: 26th March 1997
Producer: David Coverdale
Singles: 'Too Many Tears', 'Don't Fade Away', 'All in the Name of Love'

"I like 'Don't Fade Away' & 'No More Tears', nice song... Thanks DC."
Estiarto Coverdale (South Jakarta, Indonesia)

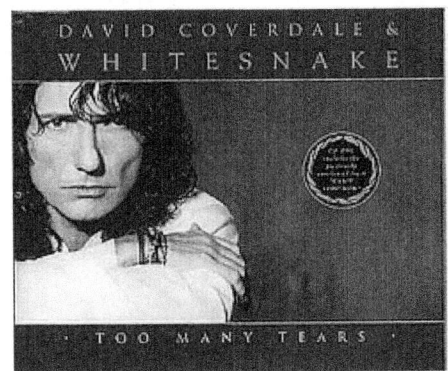

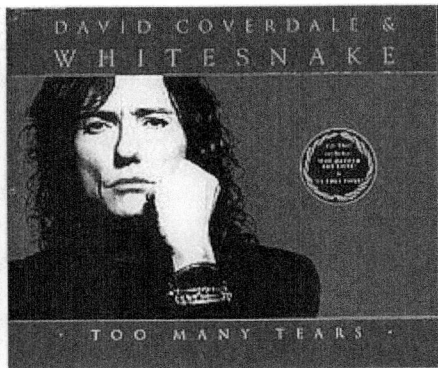

"Hair gone wild."
Robert Kelly (Canada)

"Great bluesy album. Was the music for my travel in Cuba '98."
Ale G. Gabanotto (Mogliano Veneto, Italy)

*"Step back from Heavy Metal.
Great Guitarwork from Adrian Vandenberg."*
Winfried Havermeier (Lüdinghausen, Germany)

"1st time I saw Whitesnake on tour. They were brilliant."
John Austin (Irvine, North Ayrshire, Scotland, UK)

"ONE OF THEIR BEST ALBUMS."
Leyton Davies (Sheffield, UK)

*"After the bells and whistles of and everything else of '**Slip of the Tongue**' it was great to hear Coverdale and Co. get back to their roots with the Blues. Suits his voice.
The guy can scream and holler with the best of em, but his rich tone stands out here."*
Paul Whitehead (Leeds, UK)

"One of the most UNDER RATED albums of all time."
Steve Arnold (Sydney, Australia)

"There hasn't been an official vinyl release of this album yet."
Jörg Planer (Jena, Germany)

*"Easy on the ear album...only have it on cd!!!
Did see them twice on this tour in Manchester... Not the most memorable of gigs if I may say so...???"*
Shaun Maher (Liverpool, UK)

"I still like this album. It's not brilliant but it ok."
Jayne Chadwick (UK)

Netherlands

(Including – 'My Favourite Whitesnake Concert')

"In 1987 I hear that Adrian Vandenberg would be invited by David Coverdale to play the guitar solo of '**Here I Go Again**' (remake 1987) and it made me so proud that he was playin' on that album.
But why he?
Well the answer is simple Adrian has it all - the skills for a good guitar player... Adrian has a lot of friends in the world.
And my story is I met Adrian a couple of times and he is a normal guy from the Netherlands.
(his friends are, Steve Vai, Rudy Sarzo and David Coverdale)."
Gerrit de Witt (Zutphen)

Good to Be Bad

1) Best Years..............................5:16
2) Can You Hear the Wind Blow.........5:03
3) Call on Me...............................5:01
4) All I Want All I Need..................5:40
5) Good to Be Bad........................5:13
6) All for Love.............................5:13
7) Summer Rain...........................6:10
8) Lay Down Your Love..................6:01
9) A Fool in Love.........................5:50
10) Got What You Need..................4:15
11) Til the End of Time...................5:32

Release Date: 21st April 2008
Producer: The Brutal Brothers – David Coverdale, Doug Aldrich, Michael McIntyre
Singles: 'Lay Down Your Love', 'All for Love', 'Summer Rain'

"Great come back album with a kick ass line up."
Paul Whitehead (Leeds, UK)

*"**Best Years**' - best song for ages. Great solo and chorus."*
Kevin R. Halewood (Aukland, New Zealand)

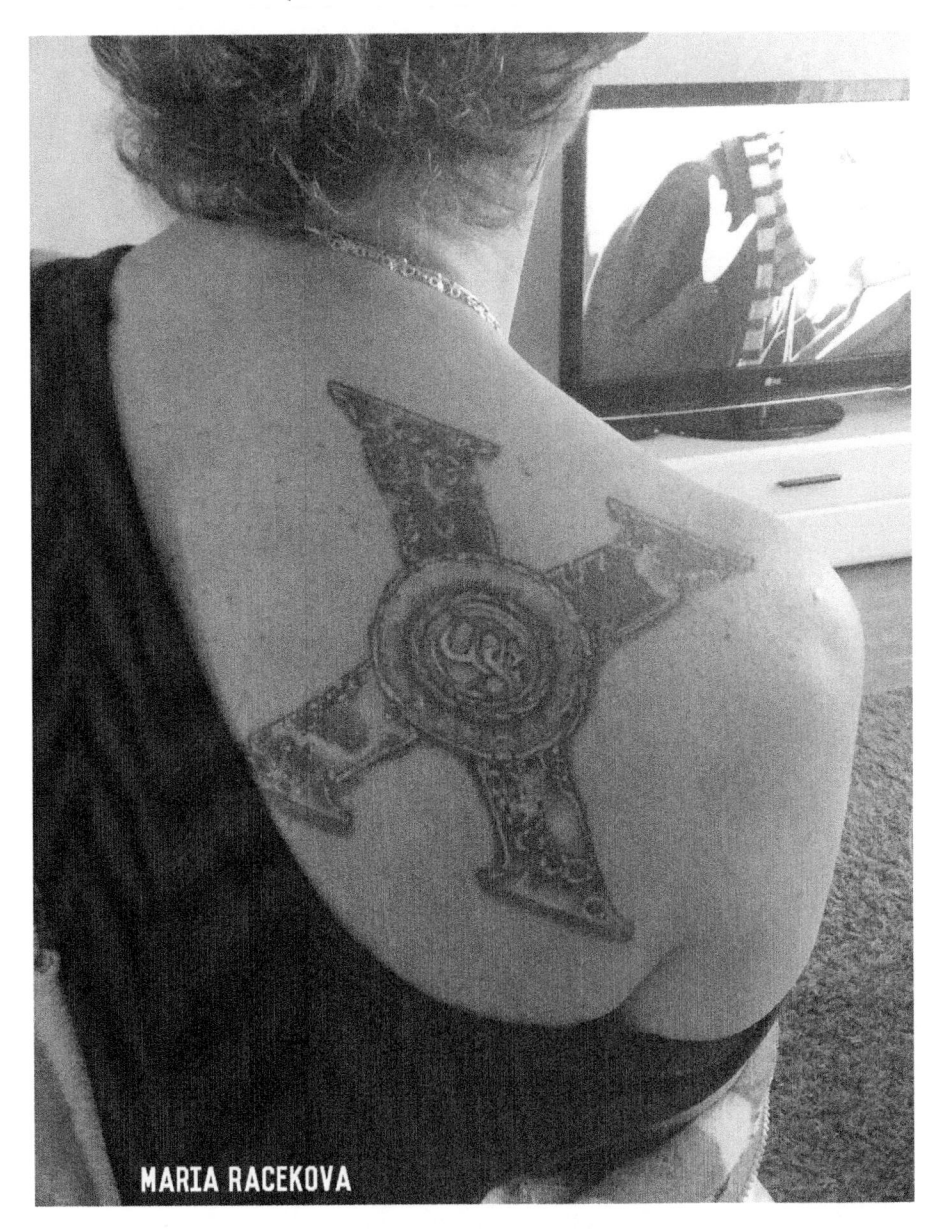

MARIA RACEKOVA

"Good album... Like the mix on this, heavy but subtle with it."
Shaun Maher (Liverpool, UK)

"The worst drummer that has passed through the 'snake's line-ups?"
Rodolfo Bombachi (Buenos Aires, Argentina)

"Why isn't it on spotify yet?"
Marcus Martins (Caçapava, Brazil)

The Fan Have Their Say #13 Whitesnake: In the Still of the Night...

New Zealand

(Including – 'My Favourite Whitesnake Concert')

"Seen Whitesnake, a few times - Donnington as headliners was great, Coverdale made my night. Then saw them in Wellington as support for Ozzy and danced the show away. Loved David since Deep Purple days and pray he will visit New Zealand again."
Lyn Smith (Waitakere)

Westpac Stadium, Wellington
23rd March 2008

Best Years
Fool For Your Loving
Love Ain't No Stranger
Is This Love
Here I Go Again
Can You Hear the Wind Blow
Give Me All Your Love
Crying in the Rain
Lay Down Your Love
Still of the Night

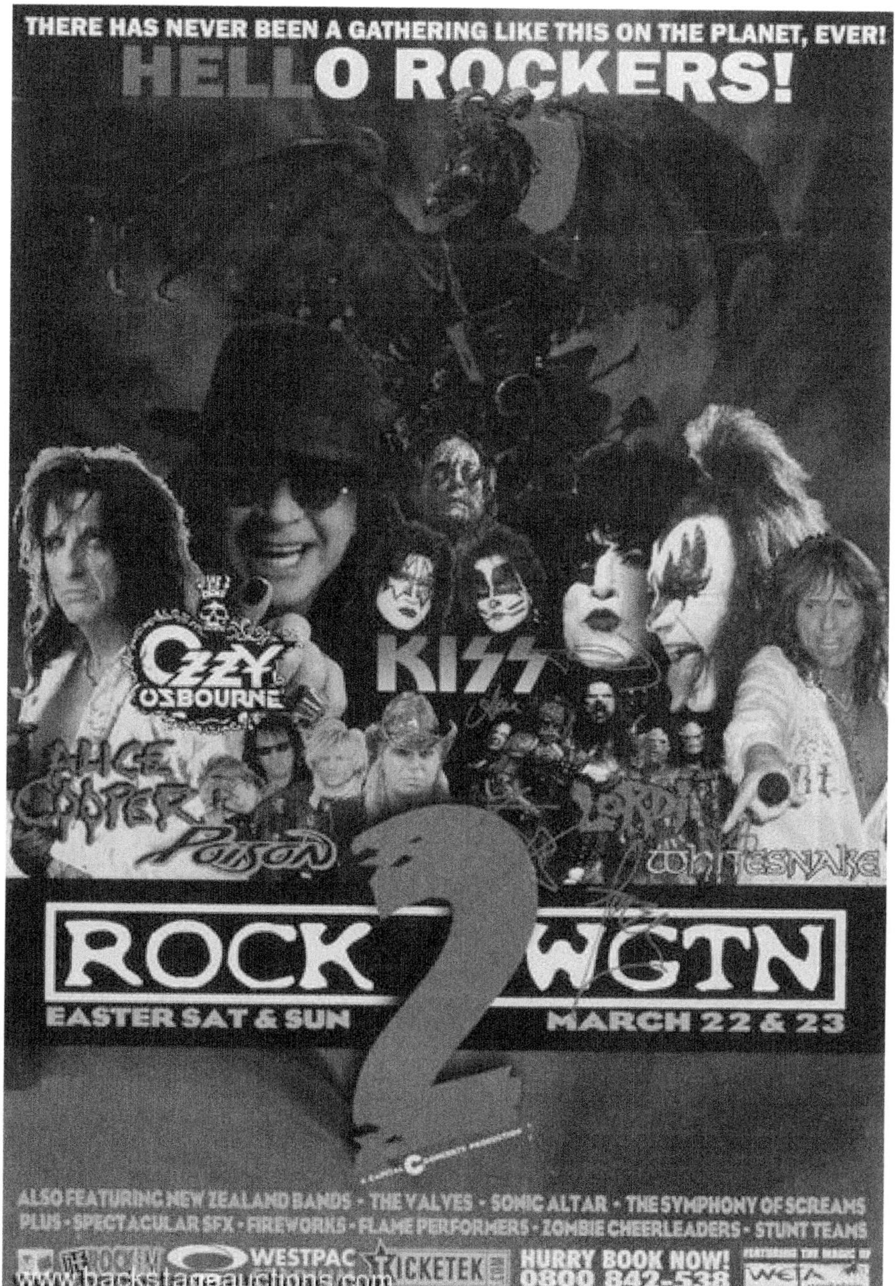
THERE HAS NEVER BEEN A GATHERING LIKE THIS ON THE PLANET, EVER!
HELLO ROCKERS!
OZZY OSBOURNE
KISS
POISON
WHITESNAKE
ROCK 2 WGTN
EASTER SAT & SUN
MARCH 22 & 23
ALSO FEATURING NEW ZEALAND BANDS · THE VALVES · SONIC ALTAR · THE SYMPHONY OF SCREAMS
PLUS · SPECTACULAR SFX · FIREWORKS · FLAME PERFORMERS · ZOMBIE CHEERLEADERS · STUNT TEAMS
WESTPAC
TICKETEK
HURRY BOOK NOW!
0800 842-538
www.backstageauctions.com

Norway

(Including – 'My Favourite Whitesnake Concert')

"Liverpool '84 no question."
Paul Murphy (Husa)

Royal Court Theatre, Liverpool 24th February 1984

Gambler
Guilty of Love
Ready an' Willing
Love Ain't No Stranger
Here I Go Again
Slow an' Easy
Crying in the Rain / Soldier of Fortune
Ain't No Love in the Heart of the City
Fool For Your Loving
Need Your Love So Bad / Thank You Blues
Slide It In
Don't Break My Heart Again
We Wish You Well

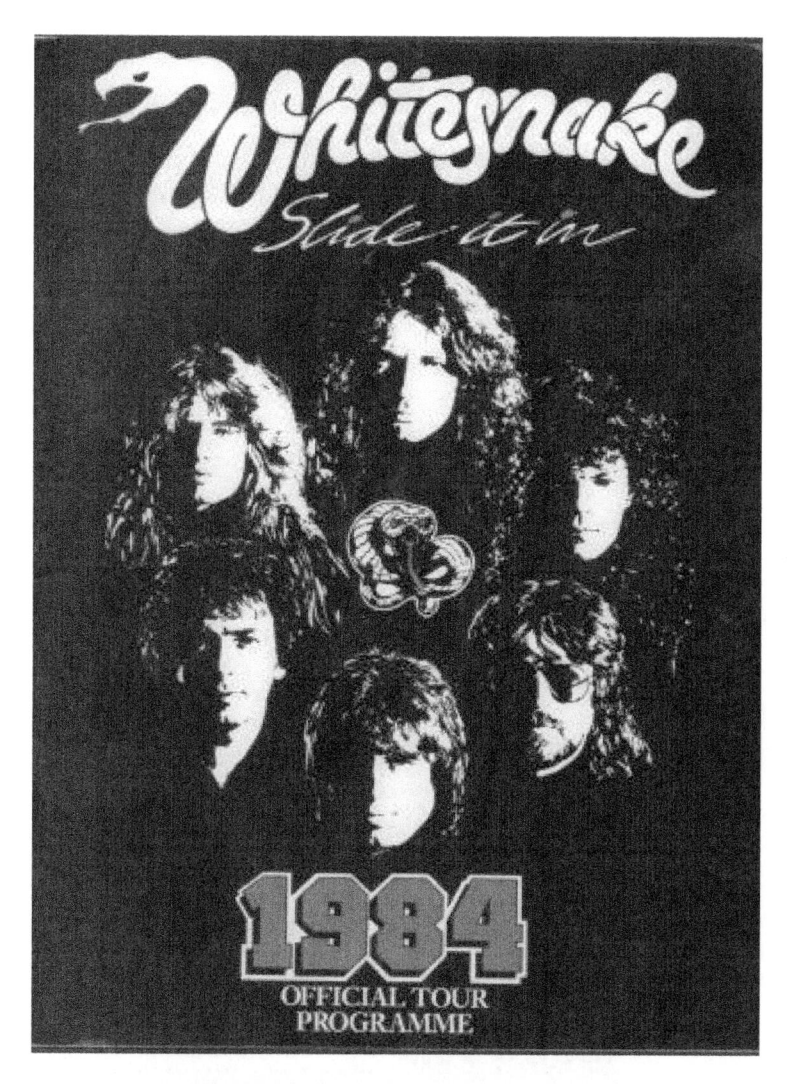

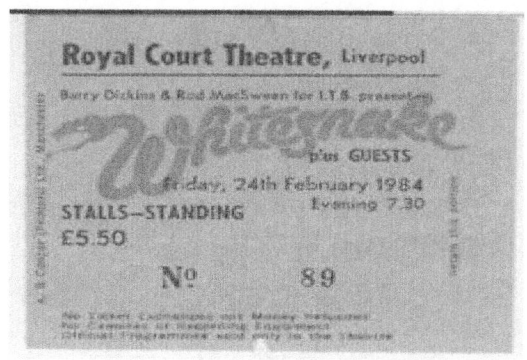

The Fan Have Their Say #13 Whitesnake: In the Still of the Night...

Forevermore

1) Steal Your Heart Away..................5:18
2) All Out of Luck..........................5:28
3) Love Will Set You Free.................3:52
4) Easier Said Than Done.................5:13
5) Tell Me How.............................4:41
6) I Need You (Shine a Light)............3:49
7) One of These Days......................4:53
8) Love and Treat Me Right..............4:14
9) Dogs in the Street.....................3:48
10) Fare Thee Well.........................5:18
11) Whipping Boy Blues...................5:02
12) My Evil Ways...........................4:33
13) Forevermore............................7:22

Release Date: 9th March 2011
Producer: Los Bros Brutalos – David Coverdale, Doug Aldrich, Michael McIntyre
Singles: 'Love Will Set You Free', 'One of These Days'

"I love this album."
Jayne Chadwick (Liverpool, UK)

"Impressive album...Can't fault it, great tracks, great mix...Great cover."
Shaun Maher (Liverpool, UK)

"Terrific majestic album."
Simon Marc (Argentina)

The Fan Have Their Say #13 Whitesnake: In the Still of the Night...

Spain

(Including – 'My Favourite Whitesnake Concert')

"2006 Madrid La Cubierta de Leganes, it was very warm so David asked for getting' the roof opened. And the roof opened.
And the moon was over the stage.
And they started to play '**Still of the Night**', a magic moment for everyone."
Alejo Fabian (Madrid)

Sweden

(Including – 'My Favourite Whitesnake Concert')

"Göta Lejon Stockholm May 7 1981... my first concert and still the number one concert in my heart.
Epic version of *'Mistreated'* and *'Belgian Tom's Hat Trick'*...
Two hours of magic!"
Per Karlsson (Kristinehamn)

Gota Lejon, Stockholm 7th May 1981

Walking in the Shadow of the Blues
Sweet Talker
Ready an' Willing
Don't Break My Heart Again
Till the Day I Die
Lovehunter
Mistreated
Belgian Tom's Hat Trick
Ain't No Love in the Heart of the City
Fool for Your Loving
Take Me with You
Wine, Women an' Song
We Wish You Well

The Purple Album

1) Burn……………………………….6:56
2) You Fool No One…………………….6:23
3) Love Child………………….....……..4:13
4) Sail Away……………………………4:53
5) The Gypsy……………………………5:29
6) Lady Double Dealer………………..3:59
7) Mistreated……………………..……7:39
8) Holy Man……………………………4:42
9) Might Just Take Your Life………….4:14
10) You Keep On Moving………………..5:06
11) Soldier of Fortune…………………..3:18
12) Lay Down Stay Down………………3:52
13) Stormbringer……………………….5:17

Release Date: 18th May 2015
Producer: David Coverdale, Michael McIntyre, Reb Beach
Singles: 'Stormbringer', 'Burn', Lay Down Stay Down' 'Soldier of Fortune', 'Mistreated'

*"Didn't see the point at first, but it kinda grew on me.
It was never gonna be a classic but not a bad effort...!!!"*
Shaun Maher (Liverpool, UK)

Switzerland

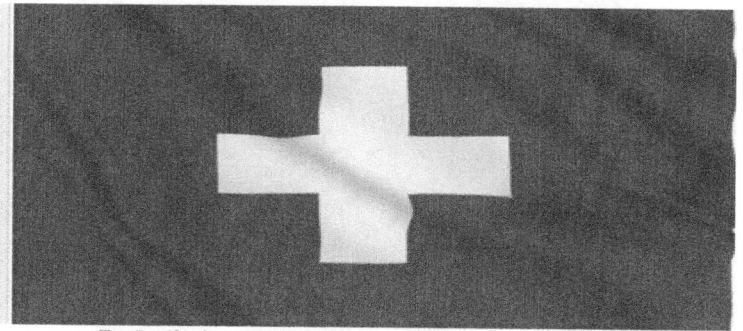

(Including – 'My Favourite Whitesnake Concert')

"November 2008 at the Albisgüetli in Zürich."
Hanspeter Baer (Switzerland)

Albisgüetli, Zurich
'Good to Be Bad' Tour
16th November 2008

Best Years
Fool For Your Loving
Can You Hear the Wind Blow
Love Ain't No Stranger
Lay Down Your Love
The Deeper the Love
Is This Love
A Fool in Love
Ain't Gonna Cry No More
Ain't No Love in the Heart of the City
Give Me All Your Love
Here I Go Again
Soldier of Fortune
Still of the Night

Flesh & Blood

1) Good to See You Again...................3:42
2) Gonna Be Alright..........................3:51
3) Shut Up & Kiss Me........................3:37
4) Hey You (You Make Me Rock)............5:29
5) Always & Forever.........................3:53
6) When I Think of You (Colour Me Blue)..3:52
7) Trouble Is Your Middle Name............4:17
8) Flesh & Blood.............................5:18
9) Well I Never..............................4:01
10) Heart of Stone...........................6:42
11) Get Up....................................4:45
12) After All.................................3:47
13) Sands of Time...........................6:08

Release Date: 10ᵗʰ May 2019
Producer: David Coverdale / Reb Beach / Joel Hoekstra
Michale McIntyre
Singles: 'Shut Up & Kiss Me',
'Trouble Is Your Middle Name',
'Hey You (You Make Me Rock)

"Coverdale and Co. show they can still cut it. Joel Hoekstra shows just how well he has fitted in after replacing Doug Aldrich."
Paul Whitehead (Leeds, UK)

"A grower...!!!"
Shaun Maher (Liverpool)

"I was standing there wondering why the snake was brown?"
Reading Eagle (Germany)

"In my opinion, their best since **'Slip of the Tongue'***. Excellent album."*
Mark Jude (UK)

The Fan Have Their Say #13 Whitesnake: In the Still of the Night...

United Kingdom

(Including – 'My Favourite Whitesnake Concert')

"Sometimes a line up change can breathe new life into a band but not these guys, when they went all 'American' around '87 they lost something."
Dean Beechey (UK)

*"I had followed David Coverdale's path, after he left Deep Purple, having his solo albums that he released, '**Whitesnake**' and '**Northwinds**', different, but worthy listening.*
*I then managed to pick up a white vinyl '**Snakebite EP**', which years later, Bernie very kindly signed for me, and I was hooked, buying all the albums, as they came out.*
*The first time I saw them live, was the '**Lovehunter**' tour.*
After the gig, I had waited at the stage door, hoping for my programme to be signed, the group of us waiting, were led back in the theatre, (Oxford) and a few moments later, the band, minus, Micky Moody, walked across the stage, jumped into the orchestra pit, and started chatting, and signing things, it was one of my first meetings with bands, I was still fairly young, and not used to this.
*I then bumped into someone who I knew from school, but was not a friend as such. He was wearing a '**Lovehunter**' T-Shirt, and we got chatting, we became great friends, and then spent years going to all sorts of concerts all over the place.*

The first one we went to, was Whitesnake, this time in London, and we got to know the familiar signage outside the 'Hammy O'... Performing tonight, Whitesnake and the Hammersmith choir, what a feeling that was, we were the 'Hammy Choir'.

I think it was that gig, which didn't go well, it seemed very bad tempered, I think they were trying to film it, and they seemed to be getting in the way, and then Coverdale's mic broke, and he had to use Micky Moody's, which was fixed, so he didn't enjoy that, even all these years later, I have no idea what it was all about.

At the end of the evening, the band apologised, and said they would do another gig, to make up for this one. We booked tickets for the next one, and it was superb.

The thing about Whitesnake live, was just singing every song, the atmosphere was just electric, the band and the audience, were just of one, and it made for a very special night.

When Whitesnake seemed to slow down, we noticed a gig notice for a bar in Oxford, called the Dolly (the Corn Dolly, was the full name) for Bernie Marsden's Alaska, we could not believe it, here was Bernie, the man we had got used to seeing on big stages down the years, and here he was in a pub!

We got ourselves tickets, and boy what a night that was, here we were up close and personal with a global superstar, we walked out of the pub that night, convinced we had just seen the start of what was going to be a massive band, didn't quite work out like that, but those 2 albums they did, were personal favourites of mine. Once again, down the years, having seen Bernie on a number of occasions, he has signed most of these albums for me, including, his own solo albums, 'About Time Too', and 'Look at Me Now'.

I last saw Whitesnake at 'Ramblin' Man Fair' a couple of years ago, a very different band, still with hugely talented musicians, although not quite with the same 'feel'.

I have been lucky, to see Bernie live a few times now, and he is always ready to meet and chat, I have been amazed to see that he is the only person, who is there to greet you at the merch stand, when you arrive for the gig!

A few years after Cozy Powell had left Whitesnake, he was on a local radio station, in Hampshire. They had a phone in, and I was lucky enough to get to speak to him, being a big fan, I was very happy, he was having to fend off questions from disgruntled Gary Moore fans, as he was now not appearing on the upcomimg tour.

We had a bit of a chat, and during the chat, I asked him about his drum solo with Whitesnake at Donington, with the helicopters, he laughed, and said it was a nightmare, as they had to get clearance from the control tower, and timing was crictical, it was very impressive, as he performed the drum solo, with helicopters hovering, and search lights from the helicopters flashing around the crowd.

I still have this on tape, but have not played it for years, as I don't have a tape player anymore.

The DJ, was very grateful for Cozy putting himself in the firing line, he had just joined Black Sabbath, and Tony Iommi, was supposed to be on with him, but he was unwell, so had not appeared, and the phone calls, seemed to turn into a tirade of Gary Moore fans, who were not happy with him. It was a bizarre situation, I think if I remember it correctly, they thought he had walked out during rehearsals, so putting the tour at risk, when Cozy was saying that Gary had fired him, because he felt he was not up to scratch. Cozy was saying, it was a very difficult show to learn, and he thought he had done a good enough job, but Gary he said felt otherwise, so fired him.

I didn't want to talk to him about that, we had a good chat, I felt like he was the sort of bloke you like to chat to in a pub over a pint."

Roy Glancey (Tadley, Hampshire)

"First time I saw Whitesnake live, Newcastle city hall summer 1980, promoting their '**Ready an' Willing**' album. Great set list at the time, and my personal favorite line up.

I heard they were planning to close the City Hall about six years ago, but it got a reprieve. It certainly doesn't attract the big bands anymore. Possibly because ten plus tour dates in small venues is no longer viable. It is probably more cost affective playing in 5 huge areas now. Shame as the City Hall at Newcastle was my favorite place to go to a concert.

I am sure Black Sabbath with Tony Martin singing was the last concert I saw at Newcastle city hall around 1987?"

Raymond Dixon (Carlisle, Cumbria, UK)

"Manchester Apollo New Years Eve 1982...

I was only 15 years old at the time but what a night!!! Such a unique way to celebrate the New Year!"

Michael Smith (Buxton)

"**Lovehunter**' tour 1979 at the Brighton Dome. It was probably my 2nd concert I'd been too. It was a really small venue and we were really close to the front. It was a fantastic night from start to finish.

Still got the tour programme packed away. Happy memories."

David Holmes (Worthing, West Sussex)

Brighton Dome, Brighton 12th October 1979

Come On
You 'n' Me
Walking in the Shadow of the Blues
Ain't No Love in the Heart of the City
Steal Away
Mistreated
Belgian Tom's Hat Trick
Lovehunter
Lie Down (A Modern Love Song)
Take Me With You
Medicine Man
Breakdown
Whitesnake Boogie

"My tickets; I wish I'd kept them all. Donington '83. One monster show."
Michael Denney (UK)

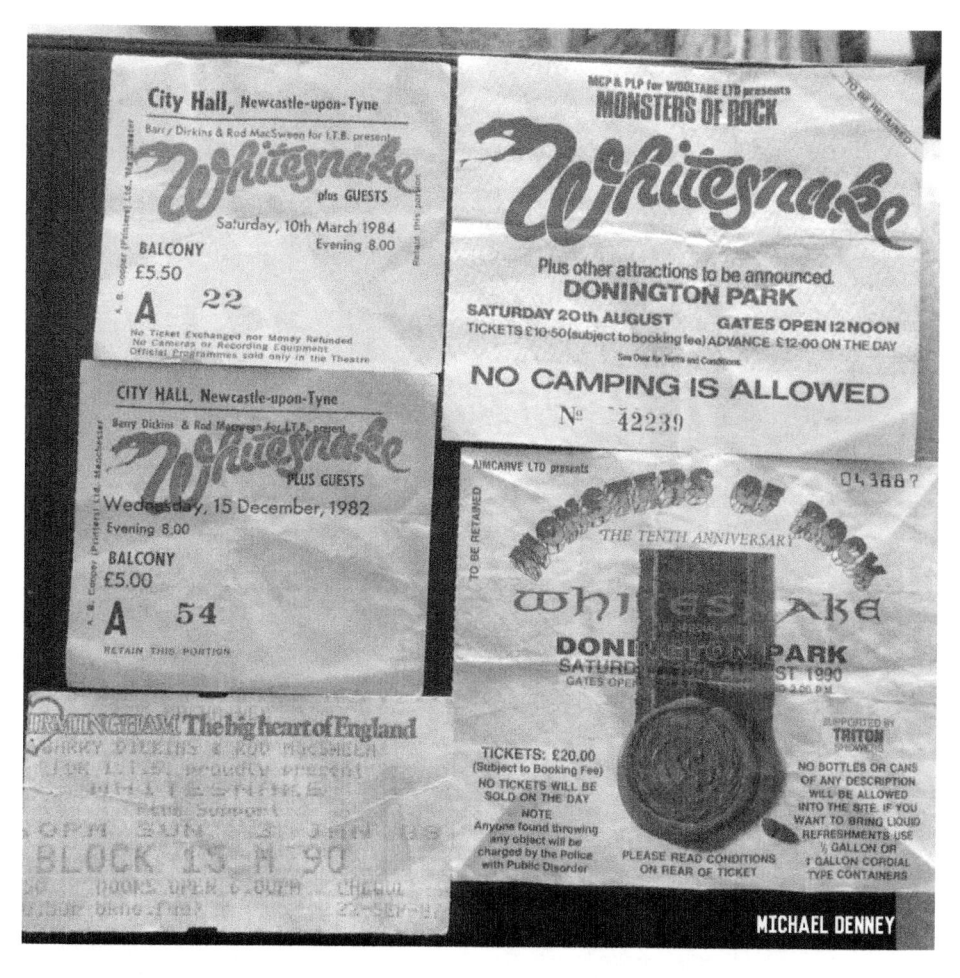

"Edinburgh Playhouse 1981.
I was 5 rows from the front, right in the middle. This was only a few months before the 'classic' line up started to fall apart, but in Edinburgh, the band were absolutely at the top of their game.
*I remember '**Mistreated**' being absolutely spine tingling. I also remember '**Would I Lie To You**' being absolutely raucous live, with a great singalong section towards the end.*
DC at this point was in a league of his own as a front man and singer, and his engagement with audiences between songs was heartfelt and genuine. This was hands down the best WS gig I ever saw, and arguably the best concert I can ever recall seeing."
Kenny Mathers (Dundee, Scotland, UK)

"81 at Donington."
Stuart Angus Malcolm Crow (Gorleston-on-Sea, Norfolk)

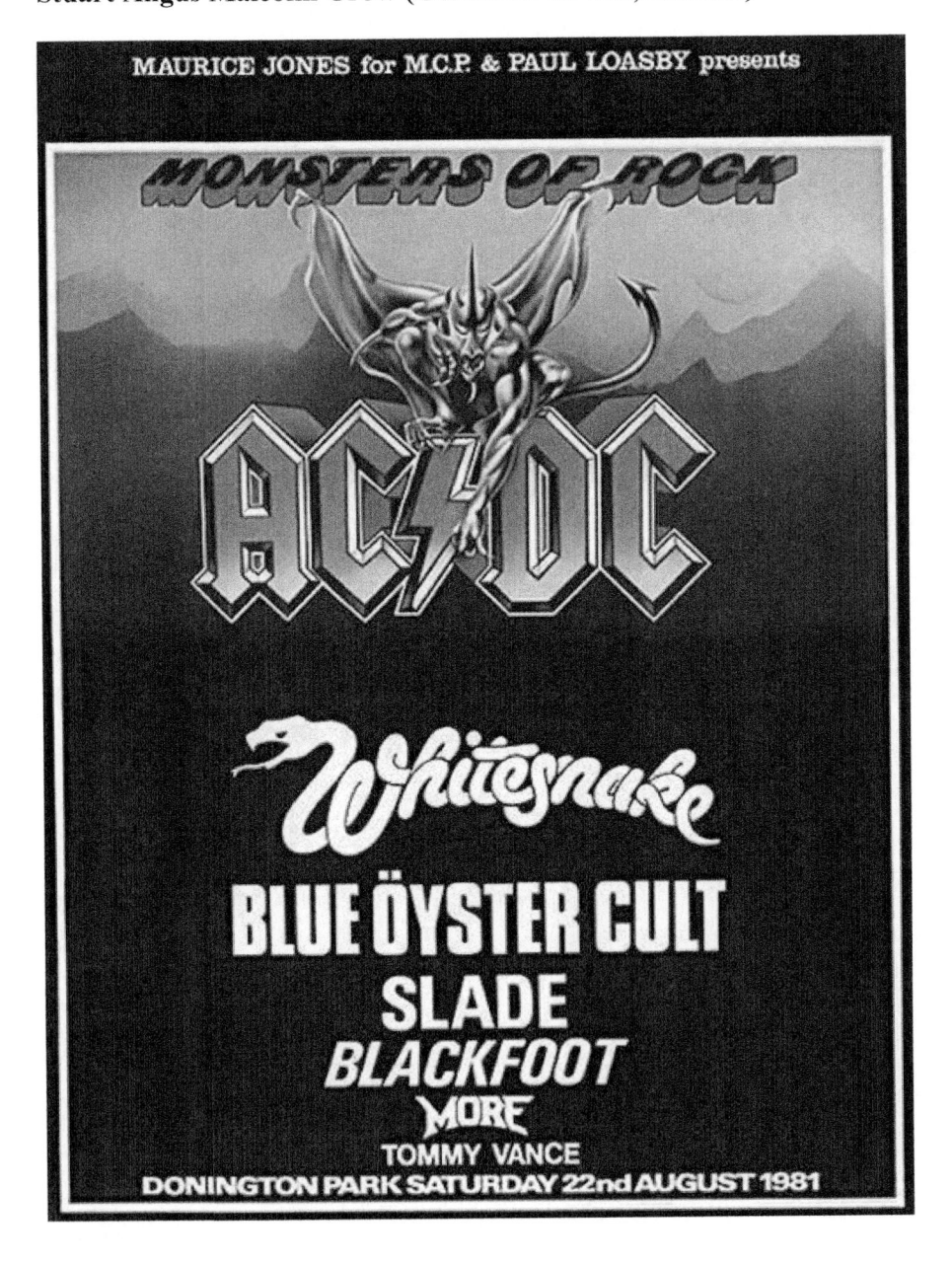

"Manchester Apollo (England) - New Year's Eve 1982."
John Buckle (Lichfield)

*"Had my best ever seats at the NEC for the '**Slide It In**' tour in 1984. On the floor and in the middle of the second row had us in prime position to watch Cozy's epic drum solo.*
The rush of heat from the flame throwers as solo reached it's climax was breath taking and it was only afterwards as I sat opposite my mate on the train home that's we realised that we had no eye brows left, just some singed black stumps instead. Had the mickey taken out of me for weeks until they grew back."
Paul Rowlands (Lutterworth)

"Without a doubt, Whitesnake's set at the Monsters Of Rock festival at Castle Donington in 1981...
ACDC were the headline band but for me personally 'Snake were the best band on the day by a country mile."
Doug Reilly (UK)

*"Donington '83... '**Slide It In**', Liverpool '84...!!!"*
Shaun Maher (Liverpool)

"Saw them 1984 (I think it was), at the Edinburgh Playhouse, I think it was. It was supposed to be 1983 but they sacked Micky Moody and eventually got Sykes in.
I was I bit upset that Mickey wasn't there, but the atmosphere was amazing.
It was a powerful performance with Cozy doing his solo spot with flames bursting up from the stage.
Some people sat down for Jon's solo spot but I loved it - crashing his Hammond to the floor and producing some great music on his own.
I wasn't sure about Sykes twiddling solos but he was pretty solid throughout.
Mel was good and did more traditional Whitesnake solos.
We had all rushed towards the stage early on then had to return to our seats. I think I spent the majority of the show in the wrong row. Ha."
Steve Marshall (UK)

*"Probably the first time I saw them. '**Lovehunter**' tour Glasgow Apollo."*
Kenny Allison (Fife)

"2002 Bournemouth BIC. Gary Moore supporting.
Whitesnake on fine form and DC's vocal performance was outstanding!"
Dave Smith Price (Frome, Somerset)

"Seen them 35 times, last one at the Cologne Palladium in July.
Best ones were gigs at Glasgow Apollo, Edinburgh playhouse, Hammersmith Odeon and outdoors in the desert at Lancaster, California. Tickets bought for Singapore in March and Glasgow Hydro in the summer.
So many great songs, great lyrics and great musicians."
Kevin McCallum (Alva, Scotland)

"2003, Bournemouth – 'Monsters of Rock' tour. Great gig. Whitesnake on their return, sounding better than they have since, Gary returning to rock one last time and Y&T were thunderous! Great night..."
Nivek Josef Kerley (UK)

"Glasgow Apollo October 1979. Met the whole band at the Albany hotel before.
The '**Ready and Willing**' tour was great as well."
Sam Bowman (UK)

"1982 Birmingham Odeon, '**Saints and Sinners**' tour."
Tony Barker (Halesowen)

"Always good anywhere in the early days loved the Reading festival shows though."
Ian Bradley (Nottingham)

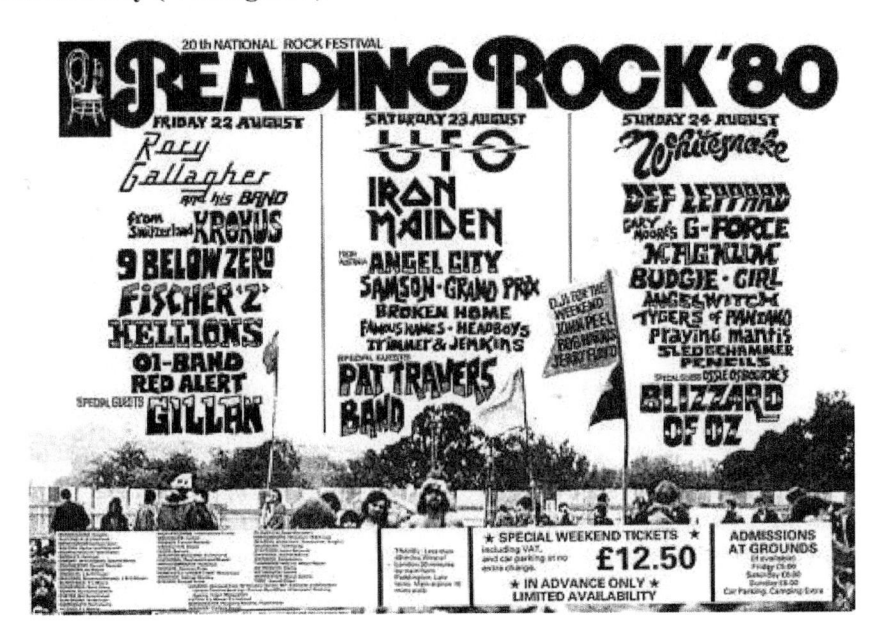

*"Too many to say.
Monsters of Rock' '83 & '90. Reading '80. Most Hammersmith Odeon (Apollo) gigs."*
Mark Jude (Colnbrook)

*"Nottingham December 2015, **'Purple'** Tour."*
Paul Collins (Skegness)

*"Hammersmith Odeon, about 1979, Gunnar Neilson benefit gig. The first time I heard '**...Heart Of The City**' live. Brilliant night."*
Simon Clarke (UK)

*"I never managed to see them until I went to Edinburgh for college.
It was 1983 and the band had just got a new album out which sounded a bit more contemporary. I was quite excited about the new direction - then they sacked Mickey Moody.
The concert was postponed until early in 1984 where we got to see the new guitarist John Sykes. I was quite impressed with his playing but didn't think his solos quite fitted in with some of the material.
Mel Galley was a bit more of the traditional blues-rock player though I never understood why Coverdale swapped Bernie Marsden for someone that was almost a clone.
The atmosphere was amazing.
Everyone ran to the front at the start. The crowd cheered and clapped to everything.
My big hero was Jon Lord and his solo was amazing. Everything had a sense of drama to it.
Cozy Powell did his solo spot with flames bursting from the stage - you could feel the heat. It was exhilarating and exhausting.
I've never been in another concert that had such an atmosphere. Everyone was up for it and singing along. Fabulous.
Some years later I saw Whitesnake again in Edinburgh on the '*Greatest Hits*' tour.
It was with a completely different band that included Warren DiMartini from Ratt. They were really impressive that night too, but the atmosphere was nothing like the show in the '80s.
I only managed to get a seat up in the balcony this time, so I took my binoculars. There was a nice moment when David spotted me looking down and looked back at me with his hand placed flat above the eyes. (You know how you do it, to show people you are looking their way?) I put the binoculars down and we grinned at each other and raised a thumb.
Some great music.
But I always wished I'd been able to see the classic line-up of Whitesnake i.e Bernie Marsden era. The nearest I got was seeing Bernie's 'Green and Blues' band at Maryport Blues Festival which had Don Airey, Neil Murray, Mickey Moody and Bernie - basically the Moody Marsden band. Fabulous musicians who still performed classic Whitesnake material.
I got a bit starstruck when I went to get a CD signed and my mouth stopped working.
"Warram mullaffle suffalong" - or something is what came out.
Mickey gave me a bit of nod with a slightly quizzical look. I've met Bernie a few times in his solo tours and he's always been a gent and played wonderfully. I wish I'd seen them all together."*
Steve Marshall (Cumbria)

The Fan Have Their Say #13 Whitesnake: In the Still of the Night...

"The Coatham Bowl, Redcar 1979."
Malcolm Walsh (Stockton-on-Tees)

"Edinburgh Playhouse '82, classic line-up! Coverdale's voice was never better, Moody & Marsden were on fire, Jon Lord... say no more!"
Alec Ainslie (Tranent, Scotland)

"Donington 1981."
Peter Rattray (UK)

"Glasgow Apollo May 1981!"
DT Gray (Scotland)

"Donington 1983 - Headliners at an amazing Monsters of Rock Festival."
Gary Clarke (UK)

"Derby Assembly Rooms (UK) 2004.
I was recovering from an illness that had taken me near death...
Opening with '**Burn/Stormbringer**'. I was blown away and I've been a fan since the very first days, having seen them some 50+ times..."
Nick Cooper (UK)

"Doncaster Outlook Club 1977, '**Back to the Roots**' tour, the first time I saw Whitesnake, then billed as 'David Coverdale's Whitesnake', Coverdale, Moody, Marsden, Murray, Dowle and Johnston on keys before he was sacked!
Tickets were £1.50!!!
Great memories."
Gaz Watts (Lincoln, Lincolnshire)

"My favorite Whitesnake concert is probably the first time I saw them live at Newcastle city hall summer 1980 on the '**Ready 'an Willing**' tour. The set list them days was very long, and it was the band's best line up imo."
Raymond Dixon (Carlisle, Cumbria)

"**Lovehunter**' tour 1979 at the Brighton dome.
It was probably my 2nd concert I'd been too. It was a really small venue and we were really close to the front.
It was a fantastic night from start to finish.
Still got the tour programme packed away. Happy memories."
David Holmes (Worthing, West Sussex)

"Reading and Hammersmith 1980, neither of which I was at sadly. Monsters Of Rock 1981, I was at that one."
Steve Gardiner (UK)

The Lyceum in London 1978. My first Whitesnake gig.
I was hooked right up until the 'Hair Metal' crap of the late '80s onwards.
Dead Fingers Talk got a right bottling. They were some punk crap band and got what they deserved.
Sadly missed the Runaways.
I've still got this cutting."
Gary Wallder (UK)

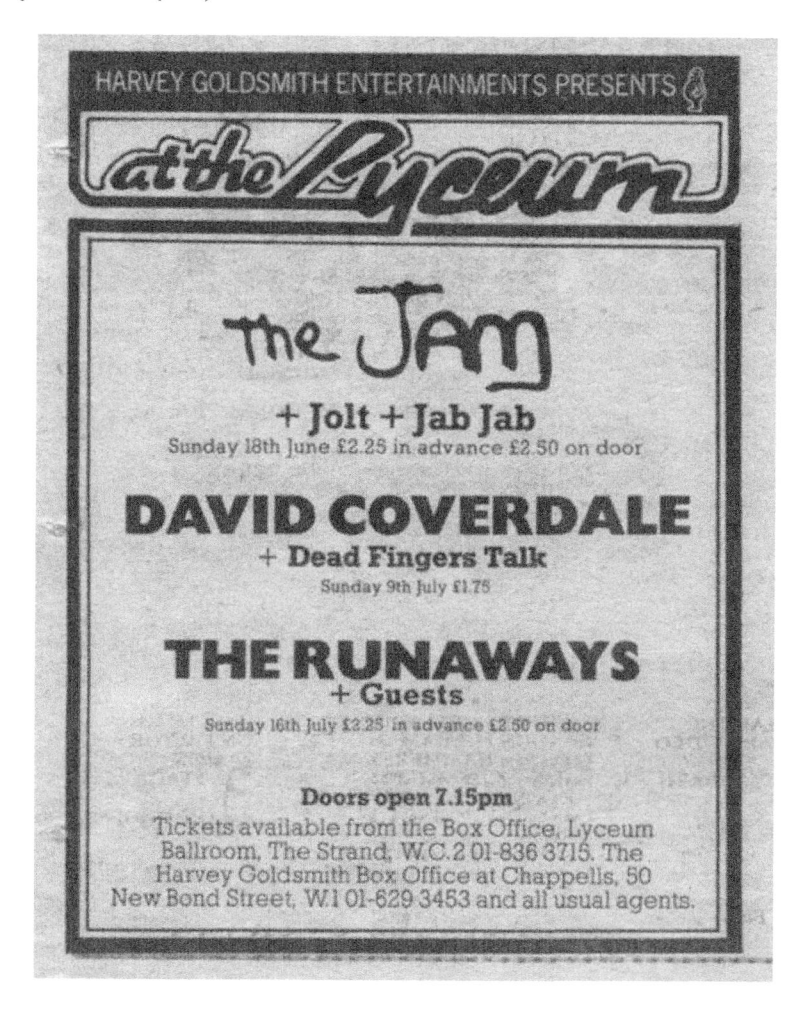

> HARVEY GOLDSMITH ENTERTAINMENTS PRESENTS
>
> **at the Lyceum**
>
> **The JAM**
> + Jolt + Jab Jab
> Sunday 18th June £2.25 in advance £2.50 on door
>
> **DAVID COVERDALE**
> + Dead Fingers Talk
> Sunday 9th July £1.75
>
> **THE RUNAWAYS**
> + Guests
> Sunday 16th July £2.25 in advance £2.50 on door
>
> Doors open 7.15pm
> Tickets available from the Box Office, Lyceum Ballroom, The Strand, W.C.2 01-836 3715. The Harvey Goldsmith Box Office at Chappells, 50 New Bond Street, W.1 01-629 3453 and all usual agents.

DAVID COVERDALE'S WHITESNAKE
Lyceum London

GALLOPING COBRAS, he can still do it. I might have been ready to write him off as a hasbeen with a half a voice, wallowing in the relics of Deep Purple. But Coverdale can still spit between your eyes ("Must we have these silly comments about Snakes? The beast should be taken seriously," Sigmund Freud).

Sunday night at the Lyceum and oh my God there's two support bands. Some persons called Radio Birdman and the worse than dreadful Dead Fingers Talk retreating battle weary from the stage, defeated by a fusilade of bottles. Come nine o'clock the place is full of Coverdale fans.

Obviously, his years with Purple have stood him in good stead. After appearing in front of huge audiences he is a master of crowd control. Plenty of pelvis thrusting for the gels and waving a beer can for the lads (welcome to chauvinists corner). He staggers backwards like a punch drunk boxer after the power of his voice seemingly knocks everything out of him. Coverdale, present and future, shows distinct promise — especially on 'Ain't No Love In The Heart Of The City'. He has a voice capable of immense power, able to stun at 20 paces or indulge in gravelly romantics.

Coverdale's combined the excitement of Purple before the beast had to be destroyed, with his own brand of knockabout brashness. Nice. **ROBIN SMITH**

Review of the Show from 'Record Mirror'

"I've seen Whitesnake in London, Sheffield, Portsmouth, Southampton & Bournemouth amongst others.
Every time I have wished to meet David, maybe one day.
Every concert left me without a voice from so much singing. The Whitesnake Choir song *'Ain't No Love…'* will always be my favourite."
Jan Stacey (Bournemouth)

*"First time I saw Whitesnake live, Newcastle City Hall summer 1980, promoting their **'Ready an' Willing'** album.*
Great set list at the time and my personal favorite line up."
Raymond Dixon (Carlisle, Cumbria, UK)

Newcastle City Hall, 'Ready an' Willing' Tour 18th June 1980

Come On
Sweet Talker
Walking in the Shadow of the Blues
Ain't Gonna Cry No More
Lovehunter
Mistreated
Soldier of Fortune
Nighthawk (Vampire Blues)
Belgian Tom's Hat Trick
Ain't No Love in the Heart of the City
Fool For Your Loving
Take Me With You
Ready an' Willing
Lie Down (A Modern Love Song)

```
CITY HALL
Northumberland Road, Newcastle upon Tyne 1

Wednesday, 18th June, 1980, at 8.00 p.m.

BARRY DICKENS & ROD McSWEEN
for I.T.B.
presents
WHITE SNAKE
Plus Support
AREA £3.50   SEAT  O   5

Booking Agents: City Hall Box Office
Northumberland Road, Newcastle upon Tyne (Tel 20007)
This Portion to be retained
```

"I've seen Whitesnake 3 times, the first was Monsters of Rock 1990. Unfortunately I never got the chance to see Whitesnake with Bernie in but I have met Bernie 3 times since."
David Wilson (Honiton, Devon)

"Colston Hall, Bristol '79 brill, then Reading Rock Fest '79."
Rob Francis (Hereford)

Reading Festival
Little John's Farm
26th August 1979

Come On
Might Just Take Your Life
Walking in the Shadow of the Blues
Ain't No Love in the Heart of the City
Steal Away
Mistreated
Soldier of Fortune
Belgian Tom's Hat Trick
Lovehunter
Breakdown
Whitesnake Boogie

*"Program from '**Trouble**' tour 1978 Manchester Freetrade Hall. Remember it well."*
Pete Townson (Kendal)

"I've seen Whitesnake in London, Sheffield, Portsmouth, Southampton & Bournemouth amongst others.
Every time I have wished to meet David, maybe one day.
*Every concert left me without a voice from so much singing. The Whitesnake Choir song '**Ain't No Love…**' will always be my favourite."*
Jan Stacey (BOURNEMOUTH)

"I went to see Whitesnake on the 'Ready an' Willing' tour at Liverpool Empire. Been a fan ever since...
Also seen them at Donington. They were fabulous."
Michelle Watson (UK)

BARBARA PARFITT

"On New Year's Eve 1987 I was lucky enough to see an amazing end of the year show at Wembley Arena in London, which finished at 10pm, so that people could still get to go their parties after the gig.
It was a brilliant concert, though the final cover of 'Tush' by ZZ Top, with the lyrics changed to 'Tits' was a bizarre ending to an otherwise perfect show.
So we watched an amazing gig as the finale to 1987, the year I bought my first house, Whitesnake released their new 'Americanised' sound on the album affectionately known as '1987' and we got to get back to Romford way before the chimes of Big Ben blasted out all across London."
Ian Carroll (Plymouth, Devon)

Wembley Arena, London, 'Whitesnake (1987) Tour' 31st December 1987

Bad Boys / Children of the Night
Slide It In
Slow an' Easy
Here I Go Again
Guilty of Love
Is This Love
Love Ain't No Stranger
Crying in the Rain
Still of the Night
Ain't No Love in the Heart of the City
Give Me All Your Love
Tush

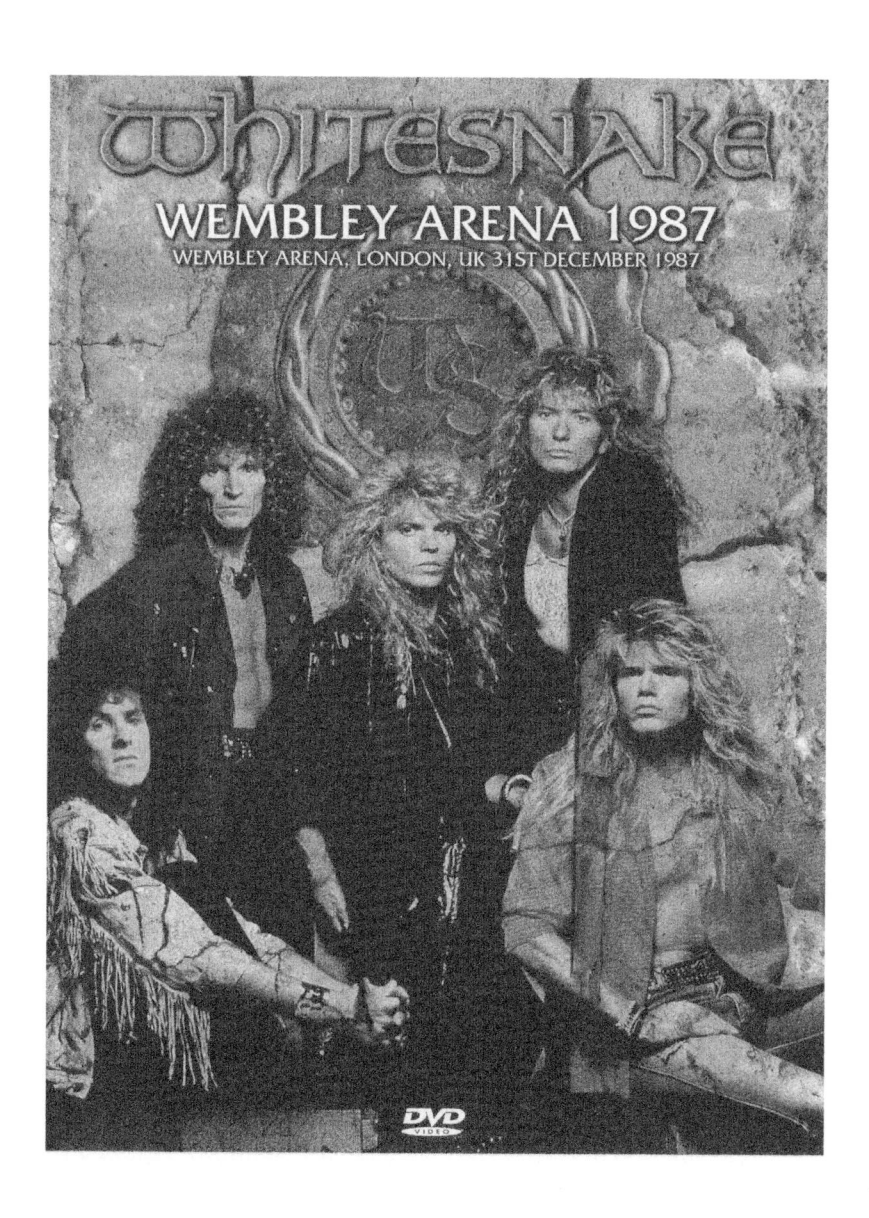

The Fan Have Their Say #13 Whitesnake: In the Still of the Night...

United States of America

(Including – 'My Favourite Whitesnake Concert')

"I have been a fan forever.
I left the hospital I was in against medical advice because I had tickets to Whitesnake in Saratoga.
Got there. I am flipping sick. I came extremely close to collapsing. Picked my head up to ask for help.
I was directly in front of their purple tour bus. Pulled everything that I had within me.
Recently died. CPR for 6 and a half minutes. Left against medical advice. Yes, I made it. Thoroughly enjoyed seeing Jason Bonham and Foreigner. But, I went to see Whitesnake, period.
Die-hard fan, yah, whatever. Got there anyway. I collapsed again and the Doctors gave me shit. I was supposed to go and see Lynyrd Skynyrd and the Outlaws the following week. Oh well.
Got to Whitesnake and that is all that mattered. Sorry, can't die right now I have tickets LOL."
Jelinda Cleggett (Wareham, Massachusetts)

*"Come Taste the Band' - when the 'Whitesnake' took over with Tommy Bolin :P - but – **'Live in the Heart of the City'** is it."*
Jason Merrill (USA)

"I was a huge Deep Purple fan with David in the band, so when Whitesnake formed Not much information was out there about them in the United States.

*I remember going into a record shop and seeing the **'Live In The Heart Of The City'** & **'Ready & Willing'** records and saw that half of Deep Purple now was Whitesnake. I snatched up both records and was floored by the songs.*

Now Jethro Tull was on a tour and just who happened to open up for them but this line-up of Whitesnake, on their first USA tour.

I saw them play at Madison Square Garden New York City. When the 'Snakes came out Coverdale totally took over & commanded that stage. Bernie Marsden & Mickey Moody's guitars sounding amazing. Ian Paice killing on the drums. Jon Lord swimming along the keys & Neil Murray keeping that bottom beat.

Strong set list" **'Come On'**, **'Sweet Talker'**, **'Walking in the Shadow of the Blues'**, **'Ain't Gonna Cry No More'**, **'Lovehunter'**, **'Ain't No Love in the Heart of the City'** *and* **'Belgian Tom's Hat Trick'**.

They played like they had something to prove to the American audience and they did, to those Hardcore Tull fans.

A show from that tour was captured in Washington show that is on the **'Box Of Snakes'** *Box Set and years after that I never missed one show no matter what the line-up was."*
Paul 'Blair' Christine (USA)

Madison Square Garden, 'Reading an' Willing Tour' 9th October 1980

Come On
Sweet Talker
Walking in the Shadow of the Blues
Ain't Gonna Cry No More
Lovehunter
Ain't No Love in the Heart of the City
Belgian Tom's Hat Trick

"The Rose in Huber Heights Ohio.
I saw you in April 2019 Best Show Ever! Please come back."
Janine Pauley (Dayton, Ohio)

"Terre Haute - It was the first and only first come first serve concert I ever attended.
I was at a one of the doors, they opened them and started taking tickets. I was second in line. As I got in I noticed everybody was running and I saw it was Mr. Coverdale's mic. I outran every single person there - 18 plus people.
I GOT RIGHT DIRECTLY IN FRONT OF DAVID'S MIKE. YOU NEVER SAW A SMILE LIKE I HAD! I OUTRAN THEM ALL. SON?GYPSY(FOR A THOUSAND YEARS).
What an evening. Didn't give a hoot about Quiet Riot who played that night too."
Rusty Lewis-LeMaster (Bloomington, Indiana)

"Best was 1987 in Philadelphia. Great White opened and then you came on and killed it...
It was Amazing...
Seen you many times, but that Philly show was insane...
WS rules."
Philip Krod Mende (Wrightstown, New Jersey)

"It was 1985 at Pine Knob Music Theater in Michigan.
*I took my 2 young children and we sat in the front row. My daughter was a beautiful 6-year old and she must have caught David's eye. When he started to sing '**Is This Love**' he motioned to the roadie to get my daughter, the roadie gently placed her on the stage.*
David reached out his arm and my daughter went right into his arm and he danced her around the stage. She was only as tall as his waist and she had her arm linked to his belt loop.
When the dance/song was over he said to the audience –
"this is going to be a cleaned up concert. There will be no more swearing."
My daughter passed away in 2015 and it was a story we told over and over during her precious lifetime. It always made the 3 of us smile. I wish it was the day of camera phones so I could have a picture but it is a very treasured memory of all of our lives.
Thanks you Mr. Coverdale for giving us this gift.
Heather Story (USA)

"Just got home from seeing Whitesnake. Well, told the good Lord that if he wanted to take me, please let me see Whitesnake first.
Well shock 'n' awe.
When this band took the stage my heart got beating real fast and I was kinda flushed.
I look to the good Lord and asked him not yet – still alive and kicking.
This band/man 'David Coverdale' killed it, as I knew they would – Rock 'n' Roll Hall of Famer, perfect in every way shape and form.
Age has nothing on this man – sensational/awesome/badass show.
Now I know why I'm single and always will be, because my 'MR.' is taken!
Love this band, love this man.
Thought I was dreaming for a couple of minutes and had to pinch myself."
Sandra Stillions (USA)

The Fan Have Their Say #13 Whitesnake: In the Still of the Night...

Album Chart Success

Date	Album	UK	US
10/1978	Trouble	50	-
01/10/1979	Lovehunter	29	-
31/05/80	Ready an' Willing	6	90
03/11/1980	Live… In the Heart of the City	5	146
11/04/1981	Come an' Get It	2	151
20/11/1982	Saints & Sinners	9	-
30/01/1984	Slide It In	9	40
07/04/1987	Whitesnake (1987)	8	2
18/11/1989	Slip of the Tongue	10	10
26/03/1997	Restless Heart	34	-
21/04/2008	Good to Be Bad	7	62
09/03/2011	Forevermore	33	49
29/04/2015	The Purple Album	18	87
10/05/2019	Flesh & Blood	7	131

The Fan Have Their Say #13 Whitesnake: In the Still of the Night...

Singles Chart Success

Year	Single	UK	US
1978	Lie Down (A Modern Love Song)	-	-
	The Time Is Right for Love	-	-
	Day Tripper	-	-
1979	Long Way Home	55	-
1980	Fool For Your Loving	13	-
	Ready an' Willing	43	-
	Sweet Talker	-	-
	Ain't No Love in the Heart of the City	51	-
1981	Don't Break My Heart Again	17	-
	Would I Lie to You	37	-
1982	Here I Go Again	34	-
	Victim of Love	-	-
	Bloody Luxury	-	-
1983	Guilty of Love	31	-
1984	Give Me More Time	29	-
	Standing in the Shadow	62	-
	Love Ain't No Stranger	44	33
	Slow an' Easy	-	17
1987	Still of the Night	16	18
	Crying in the Rain '87	-	-
	Here I Go Again '87	9	4

	Is This Love	9	13
1988	Give Me All Your Love	18	22
1989	Fool For Your Loving '89	43	2
1990	The Deeper the Love	35	4
	Now You're Gone	31	15
	Judgement Day	-	32
1994	Is This Love (reissue)	25	-
1997	Too Many Tears	46	-
	Don't Fade Away	-	-
1998	All in the Name of Love	-	-
2006	All I Want is You	-	-
2008	Lay Down Your Love	-	-
	All for Love	-	-
	Summer Rain	-	-
	Can You Hear the Wind Blow	-	-
2011	Love Will Set You Free	-	-
	One of These Days	-	-
2015	Stormbringer	-	-
	Burn	-	-
	Soldier of Fortune	-	-
2019	Shut Up & Kiss Me	-	-
	Trouble Is Your Middle Name	-	-
	Hey You (You Make Me Rock)	-	-

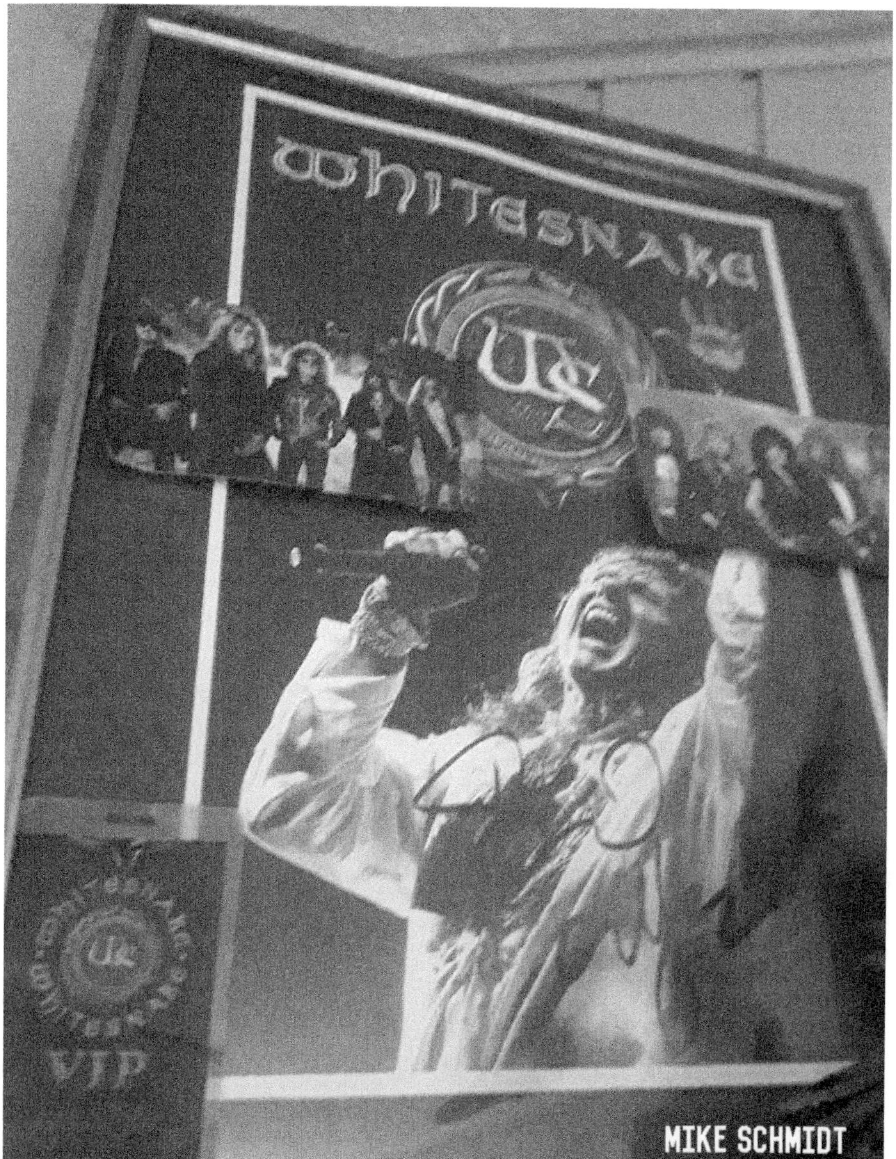
WHITESNAKE
WS
WHITESNAKE
VIP
MIKE SCHMIDT

Printed in Great Britain
by Amazon